Sunset
BOOKS

LOW-FAT PASTA

From the Editors of Sunset Books

Sunset Publishing Corporation • *Menlo Park, California*

Sunset BOOKS

President & Publisher:
Susan J. Maruyama

Director, Finance & Business Affairs:
Gary Loebner

Director, Manufacturing & Sales Service:
Lorinda Reichert

Western Regional Sales Director:
Richard A. Smeby

Eastern Regional Sales Director:
Richard M. Miller

Editorial Director:
Kenneth Winchester

Coordinating Editor:
Sarah Teter Hudson

Research & Text:
Karyn I. Lipman

Copy Editor:
Fran Feldman

Contributing Editors:
Cynthia Overbeck Bix
Sue Brownlee

Design:
Susan Sempere

Illustrations:
Dick Cole

Dietary Consultant:
Patricia Kearney, R.D.
Stanford University Hospital

Photo Stylist:
Susan Massey

Food Stylist:
Cynthia Scheer

Photographers:
Keith Ovregaard; Glenn Christiansen: 74;
Darrow M. Watt: 2, 23; Tom Wyatt: 18

•

SUNSET PUBLISHING CORPORATION

Chairman:
Robert L. Miller

President/Chief Executive Officer:
Robin Wolaner

Chief Financial Officer:
James E. Mitchell

Circulation Director:
Robert I. Gursha

Editor, Sunset Magazine:
William R. Marken

Senior Editor (Food & Entertaining):
Jerry Anne Di Vecchio

First printing October 1994
Copyright © 1994
Sunset Publishing Corporation
Menlo Park, CA 94025
First edition. All rights reserved, including
the right of reproduction in whole or
in part in any form.

ISBN 0-376-024771-1
Library of Congress
Catalog Card Number: 94-66505
Printed in the United States

Cover: Turkey Sausage with Penne (page
51); Crab with Emerald Sauce. (page 62).
Design by Image Network, Inc.
Photography by Keith Ovregaard.

PASTA — THE HEALTHFUL CHOICE

It's no wonder pasta plays such a prominent role in today's healthful eating. Low in fat and rich in complex carbohydrates, most pasta has virtually no cholesterol or sodium. But good nutrition is only part of the reason for pasta's enduring popularity. Its mild, unassertive flavor makes it the perfect foundation for fresh vegetables, succulent seafood and poultry, robust meats, legumes, cheeses, and a myriad of herbs, spices, and other flavorful ingredients.

The recipes in this book reflect both the versatility and the wholesome goodness of pasta. Soups, salads, entrées, side dishes, even desserts—all are as good tasting as they are good for you. Whether you prefer colorful spinach fettuccine, whimsically shaped farfalle, delicate strands of capellini, or tubular manicotti, you're sure to discover a wealth of dishes that load up on flavor rather than fat.

All the pasta recipes conform to the American Heart Association recommendations for fat intake. In each, fat provides less than 30% of the calories. For an explanation of the nutritional data following the recipes, see page 5.

The recipes in this book were developed and tested in the Sunset test kitchens. If you have comments or suggestions, please let us hear from you. You can write to us at the following address:

Sunset Books
Cook Book Editorial
80 Willow Road
Menlo Park, CA 94025

If you would like to order additional copies of any of our books, call us at (800) 634-3095 or check with your local bookstore.

CONTENTS

ALL ABOUT PASTA

Say "pasta," and you conjure up any number of pleasant pictures—a silken swirl of fettuccine bathed in creamy sauce, a hearty bowl of macaroni-laden minestrone, a salad of twisted rotini bright with fresh seasonal vegetables, a heaping plateful of spaghetti with meatballs. No doubt about it; pasta has universal appeal. And with the array of available shapes and sizes and the countless ways to present it, pasta is always an appropriate choice no matter what the occasion.

Varied, Versatile & Good for You

Much of the enjoyment and allure of pasta comes from the seemingly endless variety of forms it takes —dried or fresh, flavored or unflavored, long and thin or fancifully shaped (for a description of the ribbons, corkscrews, butterflies, and other pasta shapes, see pages 8–9).

Even more remarkable is pasta's versatility. With its mild, unassuming flavor, pasta is the perfect foundation for added ingredients, from peanuts to pears, tomatoes to tofu. It lends texture, body, and subtle flavor to any dish. From soup to dessert, pasta has a place in nearly every meal, whether it's a dressed-up affair or a casual family dinner.

There's yet another, equally important reason to love pasta— it's good for you! In its new Food Guide Pyramid, which establishes guidelines for today's healthy eating, the United States Department of Agriculture (USDA) recommends a diet that includes 6 to 11 servings of grain-based foods every day, foods such as pasta, breads, cereals, and rice. Along with fruits and vegetables, grains are primary sources of all-important complex carbohydrates, which provide our bodies with essential energy, vitamins, minerals, and fiber. According to the USDA, one serving of cooked pasta is about ½ cup, which means that a typical plateful of spaghetti —a cup or two—provides 2 to 4 servings of the daily recommendation.

Pasta is also low in fat and contains little or no cholesterol or sodium. Two ounces of dried pasta made without eggs have just 210 calories and less than 1 gram of fat. Just read the nutritional informa-tion on a typical package of dried pasta and you'll quickly see why pasta has such a prominent place in a low-fat diet.

Of course, to take full advantage of pasta's natural lightness, you need to keep the sauces and accompaniments light, too. Rely on fresh, nutrient-dense vegetables and fruits, hearty legumes, naturally lean poultry and seafood, and the leanest cuts of meat. Instead of using fat-laden whole-milk cheese, whole eggs, cream, oil, and butter, substitute tofu, low-fat cottage cheese, egg whites, nonfat yogurt, and low-fat or nonfat milk. In meatless dishes, pairing pasta—with or without vegetables—and legumes, cheese, or tofu produces complete, nutritious entrées.

To add flavor—robust or delicate—without adding fat, make creative use of aromatic herbs and spices, zesty vinegars, and other lean condiments. And when you cook, take advantage of today's healthy cooking methods— baking, grilling, broiling, steaming, stir-frying, steeping, and braising. All can be done with very little or no added fat.

Pasta: Plain & Fancy

Dried pasta is made simply from water, semolina flour—a special flour ground from durum wheat —and sometimes eggs. The dough is extruded through dies that produce the different pasta shapes. Then it's dried for 5 to 6 hours and packaged.

Fresh pasta is usually made from all-purpose or semolina flour, water, and eggs. It's most often formed into long noodles of various widths, from narrow tagliarini to fettuccine to lasagne, or into filled shapes

---

A Word About Our Nutritional Data

For our recipes, we provide a nutritional analysis prepared by Hill Nutrition Associates, Inc., of Florida, stating calorie count; percentage of calories from fat, carbohydrates, and protein; grams of total fat, saturated fat, carbohydrates, and protein; and milligrams of cholesterol and sodium. Generally, the analysis applies to a single serving, based on the number of servings given for each recipe and the amount of each ingredient. If a range is given for the number of servings and/or the amount of an ingredient, the analysis is based on the average of the figures given.

The nutritional analysis does not include optional ingredients or those for which no specific amount is stated. If an ingredient is listed with a substitution, the information was calculated using the first choice.

such as ravioli or tortellini. Fresh pasta is readily available at supermarkets and delicatessens and in specialty shops. Or you can make your own, either by hand or with a pasta machine.

Sometimes, puréed vegetables, herbs, and other flavorful ingredients are added to pasta dough, giving the pasta intriguing taste and eye-catching color. Basil, garlic, cracked pepper, beets, and spinach are just some of the choices. A flavored pasta can usually be substituted for a plain pasta of the same shape; just be sure the pasta flavor complements the flavor of the sauce.

COOKING PASTA

Cooking pasta perfectly every time is a snap, once you know the very simple technique. It doesn't require a lot of fancy equipment, either. A generous-size pan and a colander for draining cooked pasta are about all you need. If you'd like to make homemade pasta, you may also want to investigate the many kinds of pasta machines—both electric and hand-operated—available on the market today.

Pasta that's cooked to perfection is said to be *al dente*. This Italian phrase, which translates literally "to the tooth," describes pasta that is tender to bite but still firm and slightly chewy.

When you cook pasta, be sure to choose a large enough pan; pasta needs plenty of rapidly boiling water so it can tumble about and cook without sticking. For each 4 ounces dried pasta, bring 4 cups water to a rapid boil. Then stir the pasta into the boiling water. When you cook spaghetti or other pasta that's longer than the pan is deep (or wide), hold the bunch of pasta by one end and gently push the other end into the boiling water until the strands soften enough to submerge. Or break long strands into smaller pieces.

Keep the water boiling continuously and cook the pasta, uncovered, until tender to bite, using the time specified in the recipe or on the package as a guideline (cooking time depends on such variables as the ingredients the pasta is made from, whether it's fresh or dried, and its size, shape, and thickness, which can vary from one manufacturer to another). To test for doneness, carefully lift a piece or strand from the pan and quickly bite into it; if it's tender to bite, it's done. Pasta that breaks easily against the side of the pan when prodded with a spoon has probably been cooked too long.

To drain the pasta when it's done, carefully transfer it to a sturdy colander. If you're serving a hot dish, quickly combine the hot pasta with its accompanying sauce or other ingredients and arrange it on a serving platter or plates (you may want to heat the plates ahead of time to keep the food hot). Rinse cooked pasta in cold water only when you need to cool it for a salad.

STORING & REHEATING PASTA

Uncooked dried pasta lasts about a year; simply store it in a cool, dry place. Ideally, fresh pasta should be cooked and eaten right away. Otherwise, refrigerate it for no more than 2 days or freeze for up to 2 months; or follow the package directions.

Once pasta is cooked, you can refrigerate it unsauced for up to 3 days (if the pasta has already been tossed with sauce, the pasta will absorb the sauce's moisture and become limp). To reheat plain cooked pasta that's been refrigerated, place it in boiling water and cook for 40 to 60 seconds per 4-ounce portion. To reheat pasta in a microwave oven, place it in a microwave-safe dish, cover, and microwave on high power for about 45 seconds (for a single serving), checking for doneness every 15 seconds; if it's not heated through, stir and continue to cook. Drain reheated pasta, if necessary, and serve plain or with a sauce.

The best pasta shapes for freezing are those used in baked recipes, such as lasagne, jumbo shells, and manicotti. It's best to prepare the recipe and freeze before baking. To bake, thaw completely and bake as directed in the recipe.

Capellini (coiled)

Pappardelle

Cavatelli

Elbow macaroni

Tagliatelle

Medium-wide egg noodles

Wide egg noodles

Spaetzle

Manicotti

Lasagne

Alphabets

Rigatoni

Shells

Stellini

Penne

Orzo

Tripolini

Capellini (straight)

Vermicelli

Fusilli

Couscous

Spaghetti

Farfalle

Perciatelli

Rotini

Tortellini

Fettuccine

Ravioli

Linguine

Tortiglioni

Gemelli

Ruote

Orecchiette

Radiatore

Pasta Shapes: From A to Z

Fanciful little wheels, miniature bow ties, strands nearly as fine as threads—pasta can take a multitude of shapes. Described here are just some of the varieties available (for a look at pasta shapes, see page 7).

The terminology can be very confusing—shapes that look exactly alike may bear different names, depending on the manufacturer and even the locale in which the pasta is made or packaged. Names also vary according to the pasta's size; the clue to size is often in the ending of the Italian name. Thus, *-oni* means large, while *-ina, -ini, -iti,* and *-elle* are all diminutives, suggesting that the pasta is relatively small or thin. Various pasta shapes can also be smooth or grooved, or ridged; those that are grooved are called rigati.

In general, pasta shapes that are long, smooth, and delicate are best served with light, smooth sauces. Pasta shapes that are short and thick, or grooved, can stand up to hearty, chunkier sauces. When substituting one pasta shape for another, try to match size and thickness as closely as possible; for example, you could easily interchange medium-size shells with elbow macaroni of about the same size, or spaghetti with strands of fusilli.

ALPHABETS. A favorite with the younger set, these little letters are usually used in soups.

BUCATINI. This pasta shape is similar to spaghetti, except it's thinner and has a narrow hole through the middle (like a drinking straw).

CAPELLINI. Sometimes sold coiled, thin strands of capellini ("fine hairs" in Italian) are best with light, delicate sauces or in soups. Angel hair, or capelli d'angeli, can be used interchangeably.

CAVATELLI. These hollow, ripple-surfaced dried pasta shells are good stand-ins for elbow macaroni. They look the same as a dried product labeled gnocchi.

CONCHIGLIE/CONCHIGLIETTE. *See* Shells

COUSCOUS. A mainstay in North African and Mediterranean cuisine, these minuscule beads of pasta cook up into a fluffy, ricelike bed for meats, poultry, and vegetables.

EGG NOODLES. Available in a variety of widths, rich-tasting egg noodles are good served alone, topped with a sauce, or prepared in soups, salads, and casseroles.

ELBOW MACARONI. These short, curved tubes are available in many sizes, from tiny elbows for soup to large ones for casseroles, salads, and sauced dishes. Grooved elbows can be used in the same ways.

FARFALLE. The Italian name means "butterflies," but they're often referred to as bow ties. They add an attractive element to salads and soups, and are equally good served with a sauce.

FETTUCCINE. This classic favorite can be found fresh or dried, plain or in many different flavors, such as spinach or herb and garlic. "Small ribbons" range from ¼ to ⅜ inch wide. They're perfect with all kinds of hearty sauces—creamy or chunky, with meat, seafood, or vegetables.

FUSILLI. "Twisted spaghetti" comes in long, spiraled strands. Use this attractive shape as you would regular spaghetti or break it into smaller pieces for soups and salads.

GEMELLI. These look like two short strands of spaghetti twisted together. Sauce and serve this pasta shape as you would rotini.

GNOCCHI. Fresh gnocchi are little dumplings made from semolina flour, potatoes, or even ricotta cheese. A dried product labeled gnocchi is made from semolina flour and is hollow with fluted sides (it looks the same as cavatelli).

LASAGNE. These wide ribbons, often with rippled edges, are usually used in baked dishes. New, easy-to-use varieties need not be cooked before assembling for baking with other ingredients; they can simply be moistened slightly.

LINGUINE. Long and thin, these "little tongues" are oval shaped, halfway between a flat ribbon and a cylindrical strand. Use them as you would spaghetti.

MANICOTTI. "Little muffs" are one of the larger tube shapes available. You can find them smooth or grooved. Simply stuff them, top with a sauce, and then bake them.

MOSTACCIOLI. Two-inch-long ridged or smooth "mustaches" have diagonally cut ends and look the same as penne. They're good with a chunky meat sauce or a robust tomato sauce.

ORECCHIETTE. Cup-shaped "little ears" are perfectly designed to hold sauces and seasonings. Serve them in salads or in main dishes.

ORZO. These tiny, grainlike "barley" shapes are perfect in soups; they also appear in side dishes and main courses.

PAPPARDELLE. These inch-wide lasagne-style ribbons, with smooth or pinked edges, are traditionally served with hare in Tuscany. They're also good with other main-dish ingredients and in salads.

PENNE. Translated as "quill pens," these short tubes are cut diagonally at the ends and look just like mostaccioli. They're available smooth or grooved, which make them perfect carriers for robust, chunky sauces.

PERCIATELLI. "Small pierced" strands are like fat spaghetti with a hole lengthwise through the middle (similar to bucatini). Use them as you would spaghetti.

RADIATORE. Little "radiators" are ruffled and ridged shapes that come plain or in a variety of flavors. They add variety and interest to any dish, from soup to salad to entrée.

RAVIOLI. These familiar little pillow shapes can be stuffed with a variety of fillings, such as meat, cheese, or vegetables. Serve them with sauce or in soups or salads.

RIGATONI. "Large grooved" tubes are perfect with hearty, chunky sauces. Use them in main-course dishes for a filling meal.

RISO. This tiny pasta shape, similar to orzo, is perfect for soups and side dishes.

ROTINI. These are "little spirals," or twists; their larger cousins are called rotelle. Use them as you would medium-size elbow macaroni to perk up salads or to combine with all kinds of sauces.

RUOTE. Whimsical little "wheels" add a fun touch to soups, salads, and many other dishes.

SHELLS. Shells come in a variety of sizes, from tiny ones for soup to jumbo sizes for stuffing with cheese, meat, legumes, or vegetables. They may be smooth or grooved. Sometimes, they're referred to by their Italian names, conchiglie for large shells and conchigliette for small ones.

SPAETZLE. A feature of central European cuisine, these little droplets of egg pasta are made by rubbing a thick batter through a colander. They're usually served with pork dishes or with sauerbraten.

SPAGHETTI. This tried-and-true favorite translates from Italian to "a length of cord." Tomato-based sauces are traditional accompaniments.

STELLINI. Pretty "little stars" make their appearance with equal charm in soups, salads, and side dishes.

TAGLIATELLE. The Italian verb *tagliare* means "to cut," and tagliatelle are flat cut noodles. They're interchangeable with fettuccine. Tagliarini are narrow tagliatelle.

TORTELLINI. Available dried or fresh, flavored or plain, "little twists" are filled with a variety of ingredients, including cheese, meat, and vegetables. Serve them with sauce or in soups or salads.

TORTIGLIONI. Use these little ridged twists as you would gemelli. They're sometimes called cavatappi.

TRIPOLINI. These dainty "little bows," named to honor Italy's conquest of Tripoli, are suitable for soups and salads, or can be served with a simple sauce.

VERMICELLI. Fortunately, these are more appealing than their name, which means "little worms." They're fine strands of spaghetti, slightly thicker than capellini, sold straight or occasionally in coils.

ZITI. These "bridegrooms" are tubular macaroni, sometimes sold long but more often cut into short pieces.

SOUPS

Ahhh—soup! It's always satisfying, and even more so when made with pasta. Plump ravioli, succulent beads of orzo, tender homemade egg noodles, chunky macaroni—pasta gives soup character and substance as well as a nutritional boost. From light, fragrant first-course Garlic Soup with Ravioli to lean but full-flavored Lamb, Lentil & Couscous Soup, the tempting offerings in this chapter are guaranteed to be nourishing, healthy, and absolutely delicious!

◄ *Garlic Soup with Ravioli (recipe on page 12)*

GARLIC SOUP WITH RAVIOLI

Pictured on page 10

Preparation time: About 20 minutes

Cooking time: About 35 minutes

Long popular as a seasoning, garlic is now showing up more and more as a principal ingredient, as in this light soup. Slow cooking modifies the garlic's assertiveness.

1   head garlic
1   teaspoon salad oil
6   cups (1.4 liters) low-sodium chicken broth
1   package (about 9 oz./255 g) fresh low-fat or regular cheese ravioli or tortellini
3   tablespoons *each* finely chopped red bell pepper and green onions
¼   teaspoon Oriental sesame oil (optional)
    Cilantro

1. Peel garlic; thinly slice cloves. Heat salad oil in a nonstick frying pan over medium-low heat. Add garlic and cook, stirring often, until golden brown (about 10 minutes; do not scorch); if pan appears dry or garlic sticks to pan bottom, stir in water, 1 tablespoon at a time. Meanwhile, bring broth to a boil in a 4- to 5-quart (3.8- to 5-liter) pan over high heat. When garlic is done, pour about ½ cup (120 ml) of the broth into frying pan, stirring to loosen browned bits. Return garlic mixture to broth; reduce heat, cover, and simmer for 15 minutes.

2. Increase heat to high and bring to a boil. Separating any ravioli that are stuck together, add pasta to broth. Reduce heat and boil gently, stirring occasionally, just until pasta is tender to bite (4 to 6 minutes; or according to package directions).

3. Add bell pepper, onions, and, if desired, sesame oil and cook just until heated through (about 2 minutes). Garnish with cilantro. Makes 6 servings.

Per serving: 172 calories (25% fat, 52% carbohydrates, 23% protein), 5 g total fat (2 g saturated), 22 g carbohydrates, 10 g protein, 28 mg cholesterol, 211 mg sodium

HOT & SOUR TOFU SOUP

Preparation time: About 35 minutes

Cooking time: About 20 minutes

This soup combines the traditional flavors of Sichuan with tender strands of pasta. Season with chili oil to add heat.

8   medium-size dried shiitake mushrooms (about ¾ oz./20 g *total*)
1½   teaspoons salad oil
1   clove garlic, minced or pressed
1   tablespoon minced fresh ginger
8   cups (1.9 liters) low-sodium chicken or vegetable broth
2   ounces (55 g) dried linguine, broken into 3-inch (8-cm) pieces
1   pound (455 g) soft or regular tofu, rinsed and drained, cut into ½-inch (1-cm) cubes
3   tablespoons seasoned rice vinegar; or 3 tablespoons distilled white vinegar and 2 teaspoons sugar
5   teaspoons reduced-sodium soy sauce (or to taste)
3   tablespoons cornstarch mixed with ¼ cup (60 ml) water
4   green onions, thinly sliced
     Chili oil

1. Soak mushrooms in boiling water to cover until soft (about 20 minutes). Drain; cut off and discard coarse stems. Cut caps into thin strips; set aside.

2. Heat salad oil in a 4- to 5-quart (3.8- to 5-liter) pan over medium heat. Add garlic and ginger. Cook, stirring, until garlic is light golden (about 2 minutes); if pan appears dry or garlic sticks to pan bottom, stir in water, 1 tablespoon at a time. Add broth and mushrooms; bring to a boil over high heat. Stir in pasta; reduce heat, cover, and boil gently just until pasta is tender to bite (8 to 10 minutes; or according to package directions).

3. Add tofu, vinegar, and soy sauce. Stir cornstarch mixture; add to soup, stirring until smooth. Cook over medium-high heat, stirring, just until soup comes to a boil and thickens slightly. Add onions; ladle into bowls. Offer chili oil to add to taste. Makes 6 to 8 servings.

Per serving: 142 calories (29% fat, 50% carbohydrates, 21% protein), 5 g total fat (0.6 g saturated), 17 g carbohydrates, 7 g protein, 0 mg cholesterol, 339 mg sodium

Fresh Tomato Soup With Homemade Pasta

Preparation time: About 30 minutes

Cooking time: About 40 minutes

Chopped onions, fresh tomatoes, and tender homemade noodles transform this tomato soup into a chunky first-course offering.

1 tablespoon salad oil

2 large onions (about 1 lb./455 g *total*), chopped

3 pounds (1.35 kg) firm-ripe tomatoes (about 6 large), peeled, seeded, and chopped

3 cups (710 ml) low-sodium chicken broth

1 can (about 8 oz./230 g) tomato sauce

1 tablespoon chopped fresh oregano or 1 teaspoon dried oregano

½ teaspoon ground cumin

4 ounces (115 g) Egg Pasta or Food Processor Pasta (pages 20–21), cut for fettuccine, or purchased fresh fettuccine

2 tablespoons dry sherry (or to taste)

Oregano sprigs

Freshly grated Parmesan cheese

Salt and pepper

1. Heat oil in a 4- to 5-quart (3.8- to 5-liter) pan over medium-high heat. Add onions and cook, stirring often, until soft (about 10 minutes); if pan appears dry or onions stick to pan bottom, stir in water, 1 tablespoon at a time.

2. Add tomatoes, broth, tomato sauce, chopped oregano, and cumin. Bring to a boil; reduce heat, cover, and simmer until tomatoes are soft (about 15 minutes).

3. Remove 4 cups (950 ml) of the mixture and whirl in a blender or food processor, a portion at a time, until puréed. Return to pan; bring to a boil over high heat. Meanwhile, cut pasta into 3-inch (8-cm) lengths.

4. Stir in pasta; reduce heat, cover, and boil gently just until pasta is tender to bite (1 to 3 minutes; or according to package directions).

5. Remove pan from heat and add sherry. Ladle soup into bowls. Garnish with oregano sprigs. Offer cheese, salt, and pepper to add to taste. Makes 6 servings.

Per serving: 175 calories (23% fat, 64% carbohydrates, 13% protein), 5 g total fat (0.8 g saturated), 29 g carbohydrates, 6 g protein, 19 mg cholesterol, 283 mg sodium

Tortellini-Escarole Soup

Preparation time: About 20 minutes

Cooking time: About 25 minutes

Once hard to find, filled pasta is now readily available in many supermarkets, as well as in pasta shops and delicatessens. In this recipe, tortellini float in chicken broth along with shredded escarole and other vegetables. Nutmeg and lemon enhance the soup's flavors.

1 tablespoon olive oil

1 large onion (about 8 oz./230 g), chopped

2 large carrots (about 8 oz./230 g *total*), chopped

1 strip lemon zest (colored part of peel), about ¼ inch by 4 inches (6 mm by 10 cm)

10 cups (2.4 liters) low-sodium chicken broth

1 package (about 9 oz./255 g) fresh cheese or meat tortellini or ravioli

1 package (about 10 oz./285 g) frozen tiny peas, thawed

8 ounces/230 g (about 6 cups) shredded escarole

Freshly grated or ground nutmeg

Lemon wedges

Salt

1. Heat oil in a 5- to 6-quart (5- to 6-liter) pan over medium-high heat. Add onion, carrots, and lemon zest. Cook, stirring, until onion is soft (5 to 8 minutes).

2. Add broth and bring to a boil over high heat. Add pasta; reduce heat and boil gently, stirring occasionally, just until pasta is tender to bite (4 to 6 minutes; or according to package directions).

3. Stir in peas and escarole; cook just until escarole is wilted (1 to 2 minutes). Remove and discard zest.

4. Ladle soup into bowls. Dust generously with nutmeg. Offer lemon wedges and salt to add to taste. Makes 8 servings.

Per serving: 198 calories (24% fat, 54% carbohydrates, 22% protein), 5 g total fat (0.8 g saturated), 27 g carbohydrates, 11 g protein, 18 mg cholesterol, 273 mg sodium

GINGERED SHRIMP & CAPELLINI SOUP

Preparation time: About 30 minutes	

Cooking time: About 10 minutes	

Steeping—cooking food in hot liquid off the heat—helps preserve delicate textures and flavors. In this easy main-dish soup, shrimp are quickly steeped in a ginger-infused broth.

- 6 **cups (1.4 liters) low-sodium chicken broth**
- 2 **tablespoons minced fresh ginger**
- 12 **ounces (340 g) extra-large shrimp (26 to 30 per lb.), shelled and deveined**
- 2 **ounces (55 g) dried capellini, broken into 2-inch (5-cm) pieces**
- 1 **package (about 10 oz./285 g) frozen tiny peas, thawed**
- ½ **cup (50 g) thinly sliced green onions**

  Fish sauce (*nam pla* or *nuoc mam*), oyster sauce, or reduced-sodium soy sauce

1. Combine broth and ginger in a 4- to 5-quart (3.8- to 5-liter) pan. Cover and bring to a boil over high heat. Quickly stir in shrimp and pasta; cover, immediately remove pan from heat, and let stand for 4 minutes (do not uncover). Check shrimp for doneness (shrimp should be opaque but moist-looking in center of thickest part; cut to test). If shrimp are still translucent, cover and let stand until done, checking at 2-minute intervals.

2. Add peas, cover, and let stand until heated through (about 3 minutes).

3. Stir in onions and ladle soup into bowls. Offer fish sauce to add to taste. Makes 4 to 6 servings.

Per serving: 179 calories (16% fat, 42% carbohydrates, 42% protein), 3 g total fat (0.7 g saturated), 18 g carbohydrates, 18 g protein, 84 mg cholesterol, 225 mg sodium

SPRING VEGETABLE SOUP WITH SHELLS

Pictured on facing page

Preparation time: About 25 minutes	

Cooking time: About 15 minutes	

Fresh and light, this quick-to-make soup takes advantage of crunchy, sweet fresh asparagus. Each bowlful is enriched with a generous helping of seasoned shrimp.

- 8 **cups (1.9 liters) low-sodium chicken broth**
- 2 **cups (220 g) diced carrots**
- 4 **ounces/115 g (about 1 cup) dried small shell-shaped pasta**
- 2 **cups (270 g) thinly sliced asparagus**
- 1 **package (about 10 oz./285 g) frozen tiny peas**
- 1¼ **to 1½ pounds (565 to 680 g) tiny cooked shrimp**
- ½ **cup (50 g) thinly sliced green onions**
- ¼ **cup (15 g) minced parsley**

  Parsley sprigs (optional)

  Salt and pepper

1. Bring broth to a boil in a 5- to 6-quart (5- to 6-liter) pan over high heat. Stir in carrots and pasta; reduce heat, cover, and boil gently just until carrots and pasta are tender to bite (8 to 10 minutes; or according to package directions).

2. Add asparagus and peas; cook until heated through (about 2 minutes). Remove from heat and keep warm.

3. Combine shrimp, onions, and minced parsley in a small bowl. Ladle soup into bowls and spoon in shrimp mixture, dividing evenly. Garnish with parsley sprigs, if desired. Offer salt and pepper to add to taste. Makes 8 to 10 servings.

Per serving: 183 calories (12% fat, 41% carbohydrates, 47% protein), 3 g total fat (0.6 g saturated), 18 g carbohydrates, 21 g protein, 136 mg cholesterol, 257 mg sodium

Spring Vegetable Soup with Shells (recipe above) ▶

CHICKEN NOODLE SOUP

Preparation time: About 20 minutes

Cooking time: About 25 minutes

Fresh zucchini and tomato enliven not only the appearance but also the flavor of traditional chicken soup.

- 1½ teaspoons salad oil
- 1 large onion (about 8 oz./230 g), chopped
- 6 cups (1.4 liters) low-sodium chicken broth
- 3 cloves garlic, minced or pressed
- ½ teaspoon dried thyme
- ¼ teaspoon pepper
- 3 large carrots (about 12 oz./340 g *total*), thinly sliced
- ½ cup (60 g) chopped celery
- 4 ounces (115 g) Egg Pasta or Food Processor Pasta (pages 20–21), cut into wide 3-inch-long (8-cm-long) noodles, or 3 ounces (85 g) dried wide egg noodles
- 3 cups (420 g) shredded cooked chicken
- 1 small zucchini (about 3 oz./85 g), chopped
- 1 medium-size tomato (about 5 oz./140 g), peeled, seeded, and chopped
- 2 tablespoons chopped parsley

1. Heat oil in a 4- to 5-quart (3.8- to 5-liter) pan over medium-high heat. Add onion and cook, stirring often, until onion is soft (about 5 minutes); if pan appears dry or onion sticks to pan bottom, stir in water, 1 tablespoon at a time.

2. Add broth, garlic, thyme, and pepper; bring to a boil. Stir in carrots, celery, and, if used, dried pasta; reduce heat, cover, and boil gently just until carrots are barely tender to bite (about 10 minutes). Stir homemade pasta, if used, into pan and cook just until tender to bite (1 to 3 minutes).

3. Stir in chicken, zucchini, and tomato; heat until steaming. Garnish with parsley. Makes 6 servings.

Per serving: 271 calories (29% fat, 32% carbohydrates, 39% protein), 9 g total fat (2 g saturated), 22 g carbohydrates, 26 g protein, 81 mg cholesterol, 152 mg sodium

RUOTE & MEATBALL SOUP

Preparation time: About 30 minutes

Cooking time: About 30 minutes

Meatballs made from ground turkey float in a peanut-flavored broth enriched with spinach and pasta.

- Herbed Meatballs (recipe follows)
- 14 cups (3.4 liters) low-sodium chicken broth
- ⅓ cup (80 ml) reduced-sodium soy sauce
- ¼ cup (55 g) firmly packed brown sugar
- 3 tablespoons smooth peanut butter
- 3 to 4 tablespoons distilled white vinegar
- 10 ounces/285 g (about 4½ cups) dried ruote or other medium-size pasta shape
- 12 ounces (340 g) spinach (about 3 cups lightly packed), coarse stems removed, rinsed and drained
- ½ cup (75 g) chopped red bell pepper
- 1 teaspoon Oriental sesame oil (or to taste)
- Cilantro
- Chili oil or crushed red pepper flakes

1. Prepare Herbed Meatballs.

2. Combine broth, soy sauce, sugar, peanut butter, and vinegar in a 6- to 8-quart (6- to 8-liter) pan. Bring to a boil over high heat, stirring occasionally with a whisk. Stir in meatballs and pasta; reduce heat and boil gently just until pasta is tender to bite (8 to 10 minutes; or according to package directions).

3. Add spinach and bell pepper. Cook just until heated through (about 3 minutes). Add sesame oil and ladle into bowls. Garnish with cilantro. Offer chili oil to add to taste. Makes 8 to 10 servings.

HERBED MEATBALLS. In a large bowl, combine 1 pound (455 g) **fresh ground turkey,** ½ cup (85 g) cooked **couscous,** ¼ cup (30 g) **all-purpose flour,** ¼ cup (60 ml) **water,** and ½ teaspoon **ground coriander** or dried basil. Mix well. Shape into 1- to 1½-inch (2.5- to 3.5-cm) balls. Place balls slightly apart in a lightly oiled 10- by 15-inch (25- by 38-cm) baking pan. Bake in a 450°F (230°C) oven until well browned (about 15 minutes). Pour off any fat. Keep warm.

Per serving: 347 calories (29% fat, 47% carbohydrates, 24% protein), 11 g total fat (3 g saturated), 40 g carbohydrates, 21 g protein, 25 mg cholesterol, 526 mg sodium

Tomato, Beef & Orzo Soup

Preparation time: About 25 minutes

Cooking time: About 1⅓ hours

Lean beef contributes full flavor and heartiness to a tomato-based soup enriched with orzo.

- 1 teaspoon olive oil or salad oil
- 1 pound (455 g) lean boneless beef, cut into ¾-inch (2-cm) chunks

    About 5 cups (1.2 liters) beef broth
- 1 small onion (about 4 oz./115 g), chopped
- 1½ teaspoons dried thyme
- 1 can (about 6 oz./170 g) tomato paste
- 4 ounces/115 g (about ⅔ cup) dried orzo or other rice-shaped pasta
- 1 large tomato (about 8 oz./230 g), chopped
- 2 tablespoons dry red wine (or to taste)

    Cilantro

    Salt and pepper

1. Heat oil in a 4- to 5-quart (3.8- to 5-liter) pan over medium heat. Add beef and cook, stirring, until browned (about 10 minutes); if pan appears dry, stir in water, 1 tablespoon at a time. Add 1 cup (240 ml) of the broth; stir to loosen browned bits. Bring to a boil over high heat; reduce heat, cover, and simmer for 30 minutes.

2. Add onion and thyme. Cook, uncovered, over medium-high heat, stirring often, until liquid has evaporated and pan drippings are richly browned (about 10 minutes). Add 4 cups (950 ml) more broth and tomato paste. Bring to a boil over high heat, stirring to loosen browned bits; reduce heat, cover, and boil gently for 20 more minutes.

3. Add pasta, cover, and continue to cook, stirring often, just until pasta is tender to bite (8 to 10 minutes; or according to package directions). Stir in tomato. If soup is too thick, add a little broth or water; if too thin, continue to simmer until thickened. Remove from heat and add wine. Ladle into bowls. Garnish with cilantro. Offer salt and pepper to add to taste. Makes 4 or 5 servings.

Per serving: 302 calories (29% fat, 38% carbohydrates, 33% protein), 10 g total fat (3 g saturated), 29 g carbohydrates, 25 g protein, 59 mg cholesterol, 1,171 mg sodium

Lamb, Lentil & Couscous Soup

Preparation time: About 20 minutes

Cooking time: About 1 hour

Lamb meatballs, lentils, and couscous produce a thick, satisfying main-course soup.

- 1 large onion (about 8 oz./230 g), chopped
- 1 tablespoon minced fresh ginger
- 1 teaspoon cumin seeds
- 1 tablespoon curry powder
- 10 cups (2.4 liters) low-sodium chicken broth
- 8 ounces/230 g (about 1¼ cups) lentils, rinsed and drained
- 1 pound (455 g) lean ground lamb
- 1 teaspoon *each* ground coriander and chili powder
- 4 ounces/115 g (about ⅔ cup) dried couscous
- ¼ cup (10 g) cilantro

    Plain nonfat yogurt

1. Combine onion, ginger, cumin, and ¼ cup (60 ml) water in a 5- to 6-quart (5- to 6-liter) pan. Cook over medium-high heat, stirring often, until liquid has evaporated and onion begins to brown. To deglaze pan, add 2 tablespoons water, stirring to loosen browned bits. Continue to cook, stirring often, until liquid has evaporated and onion begins to brown again. Repeat deglazing step, adding 2 tablespoons more water each time, until onion is light golden.

2. Reduce heat to low and add curry powder; cook, stirring, until fragrant (about 1 minute). Add broth and lentils; stir to loosen browned bits. Bring to a boil over high heat; reduce heat, cover, and simmer just until lentils are almost tender to bite (20 to 30 minutes). Meanwhile, mix lamb, coriander, and chili powder in a bowl; shape into ¾-inch (2-cm) balls.

3. Drop meatballs into soup. Stir in pasta. Cover and continue to simmer just until lamb is no longer pink in center (cut to test) and pasta is tender to bite (about 5 minutes). Ladle into bowls. Sprinkle with cilantro. Offer yogurt to add to taste. Makes 6 to 8 servings.

Per serving: 331 calories (20% fat, 46% carbohydrates, 34% protein), 7 g total fat (2 g saturated), 38 g carbohydrates, 28 g protein, 43 mg cholesterol, 133 mg sodium

ITALIAN SAUSAGE & BOW-TIE SOUP

Pictured on facing page

Preparation time: About 20 minutes

Cooking time: About 40 minutes

Homemade ultra-lean sausage and slow-cooked onions contribute rich flavor but very little fat to this whole-meal soup. The pasta looks like little bow ties; the Italians, though, call these noodles *farfalle*, or butterflies.

Low-fat Italian Sausage (recipe follows)

2 **large onions** (about 1 lb./455 g *total*), chopped

2 **cloves garlic,** minced or pressed

5 **cups** (1.2 liters) **beef broth**

1 **can** (about 28 oz./795 g) **pear-shaped tomatoes**

1½ **cups** (360 ml) **dry red wine**

1 **tablespoon** *each* **dried basil** and **sugar**

1 **medium-size green bell pepper** (about 6 oz./170 g), seeded and chopped

2 **medium-size zucchini** (about 8 oz./230 g *total*), sliced ¼ inch (6 mm) thick

5 **ounces/140 g** (about 2½ cups) **dried farfalle** (about 1½-inch/3.5-cm size)

½ **cup** (30 g) **chopped parsley**

Salt and pepper

1. Prepare Low-fat Italian Sausage.

2. Combine onions, garlic, and 1 cup (240 ml) of the broth in a 5- to 6-quart (5- to 6-liter) pan. Bring to a boil over medium-high heat and cook, stirring occasionally, until liquid has evaporated and onion mixture begins to brown (about 10 minutes). To deglaze pan, add 3 tablespoons water, stirring to loosen browned bits. Continue to cook, stirring often, until liquid has evaporated and onion mixture begins to brown again (about 1 minute). Repeat deglazing step, adding 3 tablespoons more water each time, until onion mixture is richly browned.

3. Stir in sausage and ½ cup (120 ml) more water. Cook, stirring gently, until liquid has evaporated and meat begins to brown (8 to 10 minutes).

4. Add remaining 4 cups (950 ml) broth, stirring to loosen browned bits. Stir in tomatoes (break up with a spoon) and their liquid, wine, basil, sugar, bell pepper, zucchini, and pasta. Bring to a boil over high heat;

reduce heat, cover, and simmer just until pasta is tender to bite (about 15 minutes).

5. Sprinkle soup with parsley. Offer salt and pepper to add to taste. Makes 6 servings.

LOW-FAT ITALIAN SAUSAGE. Cut 1 pound (455 g) **pork tenderloin** or boned pork loin, trimmed of fat, into 1-inch (2.5-cm) chunks. Whirl in a food processor, about half at a time, until coarsely chopped (or put through a food chopper fitted with a medium blade). In a large bowl, combine pork, ¼ cup (60 ml) **dry white wine,** 2 tablespoons chopped **parsley,** 1½ teaspoons crushed **fennel seeds,** ½ teaspoon **crushed red pepper flakes,** and 2 cloves **garlic,** minced or pressed. Mix well. Cover and refrigerate. If made ahead, refrigerate for up to a day.

Per serving: 328 calories (14% fat, 53% carbohydrates, 33% protein), 5 g total fat (1 g saturated), 38 g carbohydrates, 24 g protein, 49 mg cholesterol, 954 mg sodium

MARITATA SOUP

Preparation time: About 10 minutes

Cooking time: About 15 minutes

Lightening up the ingredients of the cheese mixture that's added to this soup reduces the calorie count without diminishing the soup's rich flavor.

12 **cups** (2.8 liters) **beef broth**

8 **ounces** (230 g) **dried vermicelli,** broken into short lengths

½ **cup** (40 g) **freshly grated Parmesan cheese**

⅓ **cup** (80 g) **Neufchâtel** or **cream cheese**

3 **large egg whites**

1. Bring broth to a boil in a 5- to 6-quart (5- to 6-liter) pan over high heat. Stir in pasta; reduce heat, cover, and simmer just until pasta is tender to bite (8 to 10 minutes). Meanwhile, beat Parmesan, Neufchâtel, and egg whites with an electric mixer or in a blender until well combined. Transfer to a tureen.

2. Pour cheese mixture into broth. Makes 8 servings.

Per serving: 192 calories (27% fat, 49% carbohydrates, 24% protein), 6 g total fat (2 g saturated), 23 g carbohydrates, 11 g protein, 11 mg cholesterol, 1,391 mg sodium

◄ *Italian Sausage & Bow-tie Soup (recipe above)*

HOMEMADE EGG PASTA

Tender, springy fresh pasta dough is perfect for noodles of all sizes. To alter the flavor and texture, you can use whole wheat or semolina flour for up to half the all-purpose flour.

Remember that the amount of liquid any flour can absorb varies with the flour's natural moisture content and with the air temperature and humidity. In fact, you won't know just how much water you need until you start working with the dough, so add water gradually, always paying close attention to the dough's texture.

Here are two recipes for making egg pasta. In the first, the dough is mixed and kneaded by hand. The second recipe utilizes the food processor, which reduces mixing time to seconds and kneading time from 10 minutes to 2 or 3 minutes. With either recipe, the dough can be rolled and cut by hand or with a pasta machine.

It's best to cook homemade pasta right away, but if you make more than you need, let it stand until dried but still pliable (30 minutes to 1 hour). Then enclose it in a plastic bag; refrigerate for up to 2 days or freeze for up to 2 months. Do not thaw the pasta before you cook it.

EGG PASTA

> **About 2 cups (250 g) all-purpose flour**
>
> 2 **large eggs**
>
> 3 **to 6 tablespoons water**

1. Mound 2 cups (250 g) of the flour on a work surface or in a large bowl and make a deep well in center. Break eggs into well. With a fork, beat eggs lightly; stir in 2 tablespoons of the water. Using a circular motion, draw in flour from sides of well. Add 1 tablespoon more water and continue to mix until flour is evenly moistened. If necessary, add more water, 1 tablespoon at a time. When dough becomes too stiff to stir easily, use your hands to finish mixing.

2. Pat dough into a ball and knead a few times to help flour absorb liquid. To knead, flatten dough ball slightly and fold farthest edge toward you. With heel of your hand, push dough away from you, sealing fold. Rotate dough a quarter turn and continue folding-pushing motion, making a turn each time.

3. Clean and lightly flour work surface.

If you plan to use a rolling pin, knead dough until smooth and elastic (about 10 minutes), adding flour if needed to prevent sticking. Cover and let rest for 20 minutes.

If you plan to use a pasta machine (manual or electric), knead dough until no longer sticky (3 to 4 minutes), adding flour if needed to prevent sticking.

4. Use a rolling pin or pasta machine to roll out and cut dough as directed on facing page. Makes 14 to 16 ounces (400 to 455 g) uncooked pasta (machine-rolled dough makes about 32 pieces lasagne or about 4 cups/640 g cooked medium-wide noodles; yield of hand-rolled pasta varies).

Per ounce: 71 calories (11% fat, 74% carbohydrates, 15% protein), 0.8 g total fat (0.2 g saturated), 13 g carbohydrates, 3 g protein, 28 mg cholesterol, 9 mg sodium

FOOD PROCESSOR PASTA

About 2 cups (250 g) all-purpose flour
2 large eggs
About ¼ cup (60 ml) water

1. Combine 2 cups (250 g) of the flour and eggs in a food processor; whirl until mixture resembles cornmeal (about 5 seconds). With motor running, pour ¼ cup (60 ml) of the water through feed tube and whirl until dough forms a ball. Dough should be well blended but not sticky. If dough feels sticky, add a little flour and whirl to blend; if it looks crumbly, add 1 or 2 teaspoons more water. If processor begins to slow down or stop (an indication that dough is properly mixed), turn off motor and proceed to next step.

2. Turn dough out onto a floured board and knead a few times just until smooth.

If you plan to use a rolling pin, cover and let rest for 20 minutes.

If you plan to use a pasta machine (manual or electric), roll out at once.

3. Use a rolling pin or pasta machine to roll out and cut dough (see below). Makes 14 to 16 ounces (400 to 455 g) uncooked pasta (machine-rolled dough makes about 32 pieces lasagne or about 4 cups/ 640 g cooked medium-wide noodles; yield of hand-rolled pasta varies).

Per ounce: 71 calories (11% fat, 74% carbohydrates, 15% protein), 0.8 g total fat (0.2 g saturated), 13 g carbohydrates, 3 g protein, 28 mg cholesterol, 9 mg sodium

PASTA BY HAND

Here's how to roll out pasta with a rolling pin and cut pasta by hand.

Rolling. Keeping unrolled portions of dough covered, use a rolling pin to roll a fourth of the dough into a rectangle about ¹⁄₁₆ inch (1.5 mm) thick (if dough is sticky, turn and flour both sides as you roll). Transfer rolled strip to a lightly floured board or cloth. Let dry, uncovered, until dough feels leathery but still pliable (5 to 10 minutes); then cover airtight with plastic wrap. Meanwhile, roll out remaining portions.

Cutting. Sprinkle one of the strips of rolled dough with flour. Starting at narrow end, roll up jelly roll fashion and cut crosswise into slices of desired width (tagliarini is about ⅛ inch/3 mm wide, fettuccine about ¼ inch/6 mm wide, lasagne about 2 inches/5 cm wide). Repeat to cut remaining portions.

PASTA BY MACHINE

These directions apply to both manual and electric pasta machines. But because machines differ slightly in size and function, you'll also want to consult the manufacturer's directions.

Kneading and rolling. Keeping unrolled dough covered, flatten a fourth of the dough slightly; flour dough and feed through widest roller setting. Fold dough into thirds and feed through rollers again. Repeat folding and rolling process 8 to 10 more times or until dough is smooth and pliable. If it feels damp or sticky, flour both sides each time dough is rolled.

Set rollers one notch closer together and feed dough through. Flour dough if it is damp or sticky. Continue to roll, setting rollers closer each time, until dough is a long strip of desired thinness. Cut strip in half crosswise for easy handling; place pieces on a lightly floured board or cloth. Let dry, uncovered, until dough feels leathery but still pliable (5 to 10 minutes); then cover airtight with plastic wrap. Meanwhile, roll out remaining portions.

Cutting. Feed each strip through medium-wide blades for fettuccine or through narrow blades for thin noodles or tagliarini. Some machines have attachments for wide and narrow lasagne; if yours doesn't, cut by hand.

Lightly flour cut pasta to keep strands separate. Toss in a loose pile or gather strands and lay in rows.

COOKING HOMEMADE PASTA

These homemade pastas cook quickly; the time depends on the thinness of the pasta. Cook in a generous quantity of boiling water just until tender to bite (1 to 3 minutes). For more on cooking pasta, see page 6.

MINESTRONE GENOVESE

Pictured on facing page

Preparation time: About 30 minutes

Cooking time: 25 to 30 minutes

Fresh vegetables, white kidney beans, and macaroni mingle in this colorful, hearty one-pot meal. Serve the soup hot or at room temperature.

     Pesto (recipe follows)
  2 large leeks (about 1¼ lbs./565 g *total*)
 12 cups (2.8 liters) low-sodium chicken broth
  2 large carrots (about 8 oz./230 g *total*), thinly sliced
  3 large stalks celery (about 12 oz./340 g *total*), thinly sliced
  2 cans (about 15 oz./425 g *each*) cannellini (white kidney beans), drained
  8 ounces/230 g (about 2 cups) dried medium-size elbow macaroni
  1 pound (455 g) yellow crookneck squash or zucchini (about 4 medium-size), cut into ½-inch (1-cm) chunks
  1 large red bell pepper (about 8 oz./230 g), seeded and cut into ½-inch (1-cm) pieces
  1 package (about 1 lb./455 g) frozen tiny peas
     Basil sprigs
     Salt and pepper

1. Prepare Pesto.

2. Cut off and discard root ends and green tops of leeks. Discard coarse outer leaves. Split leeks in half lengthwise and rinse well; thinly slice crosswise.

3. Combine leeks, broth, carrots, and celery in an 8- to 10-quart (8- to 10-liter) pan. Bring to a boil over high heat; reduce heat, cover, and simmer for 10 minutes.

4. Stir in beans, pasta, squash, and bell pepper; cover and simmer just until pasta is tender to bite (about 10 more minutes).

5. Add peas and bring to a boil. Stir ½ cup (120 ml) of the Pesto into soup. Serve hot or at room temperature. If made ahead, let cool and then cover and refrigerate for up to a day; bring to room temperature or reheat before serving.

6. Garnish with basil. Offer salt, pepper, and remaining Pesto to add to taste. Makes 10 to 12 servings.

Per serving: 277 calories (22% fat, 58% carbohydrates, 20% protein), 7 g total fat (2 g saturated), 41 g carbohydrates, 14 g protein, 3 mg cholesterol, 310 mg sodium

PESTO. In a food processor or blender, combine 2 cups (80 g) lightly packed **fresh basil**, 1 cup (about 4 oz./115 g) freshly grated **Parmesan cheese**, ¼ cup (60 ml) **olive oil**, 2 tablespoons **pine nuts** or slivered almonds, and 1 or 2 cloves **garlic.** Whirl until smooth. Season to taste with **salt.** If made ahead, cover and refrigerate for up to a day. Makes 1 cup.

VEGETABLE SOUP WITH COUSCOUS

Preparation time: About 30 minutes

Cooking time: About 55 minutes

Couscous—granular-shaped pasta made from semolina wheat—cooks in just minutes, giving this mint-infused soup extra heartiness.

  1   tablespoon olive oil
  2   ounces (55 g) pancetta or bacon, chopped
  2   cloves garlic, minced or pressed
  1   large onion (about 8 oz./230 g), chopped
  8   cups (1.9 liters) low-sodium chicken broth
  1   large russet potato (about 8 oz./230 g), peeled and diced
  2   tablespoons chopped fresh mint or 1 tablespoon dried mint
  ½   teaspoon dried oregano
  ¼   teaspoon crushed red pepper flakes (or to taste)
  2   cans (about 15 oz./425 g *each*) garbanzo beans, drained
 1½ pounds (680 g) pear-shaped (Roma-type) tomatoes (about 8 large), diced
  5   ounces/140 g (about ¾ cup) dried couscous
  1   pound (455 g) escarole, ends trimmed, cut into 3-inch (8-cm) slivers
      Freshly grated Parmesan cheese
      Salt and pepper

(Continued on page 24)

Minestrone Genovese (recipe above left) ▶

1. Heat oil in a 5- to 6-quart (5- to 6-liter) pan over medium-high heat (omit oil if using bacon). Add pancetta and cook, stirring often, until lightly browned (about 5 minutes). Add garlic and onion; cook, stirring, until onion is soft (about 5 more minutes). Drain off fat.

2. Add broth, potato, mint, oregano, and red pepper flakes. Bring to a boil; reduce heat, cover, and simmer for 30 minutes.

3. Add beans and tomatoes; return to a boil. Stir in pasta; reduce heat, cover, and simmer just until pasta is tender to bite (about 5 minutes).

4. Stir in escarole and cook just until wilted (about 1 minute). Serve hot or at room temperature. If made ahead, let cool and then cover and refrigerate for up to a day; bring to room temperature or reheat before serving.

5. Offer cheese, salt, and pepper to add to taste. Makes 6 to 8 servings.

Per serving: 305 calories (26% fat, 57% carbohydrates, 17% protein), 9 g total fat (2 g saturated), 44 g carbohydrates, 13 g protein, 5 mg cholesterol, 277 mg sodium

CHARD SOUP WITH BEANS & ORZO

Preparation time: About 40 minutes

Cooking time: About 45 minutes

Offer this flavorful and nutritious meal-in-a-bowl with a loaf of crusty Italian bread and dry white wine.

1 **pound (455 g) pear-shaped (Roma-type) tomatoes (about 5 large)**

2 **tablespoons olive oil**

1 **large onion (about 8 oz./230 g), chopped**

1 **clove garlic, minced or pressed**

2 **medium-size stalks celery (about 6 oz./170 g *total*), diced**

2 **ounces (55 g) thinly sliced prosciutto or cooked ham, slivered**

12 **cups (2.8 liters) beef broth**

2 **large carrots (about 8 oz./230 g *total*), diced**

1 **tablespoon minced fresh rosemary or 1 teaspoon dried rosemary**

1 **pound (455 g) Swiss chard, coarse stems removed**

3 **cans (about 15 oz./425 g *each*) pinto beans, drained and rinsed, or 6 cups cooked (about 3 cups/570 g dried) pinto beans, drained and rinsed**

8 **ounces (230 g) green beans, cut into 1-inch (2.5-cm) lengths**

1 **pound (455 g) zucchini (about 3 large), cut into ¾-inch (2-cm) chunks**

4 **ounces/115 g (about ⅔ cup) dried orzo or other rice-shaped pasta**

Freshly grated Parmesan cheese

Salt and pepper

1. Bring 4 cups (950 ml) water to a boil in an 8- to 10-quart (8- to 10-liter) pan over high heat. Drop tomatoes into water and cook for 1 minute. Lift out; peel and discard skin. Chop tomatoes and set aside. Discard water.

2. Heat oil in pan over medium-high heat. Add onion, garlic, celery, and prosciutto. Cook, stirring often, until onion is soft (5 to 8 minutes). Add broth, carrots, and rosemary. Bring to a boil; reduce heat, cover, and simmer for 10 minutes. Meanwhile, cut chard crosswise into ½-inch (1-cm) strips. Mash 1 can of the pinto beans (or 2 cups of the home-cooked beans).

3. Add mashed and whole pinto beans, green beans, zucchini, and tomatoes to pan; stir well. Cover and simmer for 5 more minutes.

4. Stir in chard and pasta; simmer, uncovered, just until pasta is tender to bite (about 10 more minutes). Serve hot or at room temperature. If made ahead, let cool and then cover and refrigerate for up to a day; bring to room temperature or reheat before serving.

5. Offer cheese, salt, and pepper to add to taste. Makes 10 to 12 servings.

Per serving: 212 calories (22% fat, 56% carbohydrates, 22% protein), 5 g total fat (0.6 g saturated), 31 g carbohydrates, 12 g protein, 4 mg cholesterol, 1,291 mg sodium

Floating like golden pillows in a homemade broth, delicate one-bite ravioli conceal a delectable treasure—an intense concentration of broth enhanced by Madeira.

Although the ravioli aren't complicated to make, you do have to allow time for the broth and filling to cook. Once the broth has simmered, strain it and save some for the soup. The rest is boiled down; when chilled, it becomes rigid, a suitable filling for won ton skins.

CONSOMME RAVIOLI

Preparation time: About 5 hours

Cooking time: About 6 hours

Roasted-bone Broth (recipe follows)

Consommé (recipe follows)

1 tablespoon all-purpose flour

16 **won ton skins**

Salt

2 tablespoons *each* freshly grated Parmesan cheese and thinly sliced chives

1. Prepare Roasted-bone Broth and Consommé.

2. Mix flour and 2 tablespoons water in a small bowl until smooth. Cut won ton skins in half lengthwise to make pieces about 1¾ by 3¼ inches (4.5 by 8.25 cm). Keeping remaining pieces covered, brush edges of a won ton piece with flour

mixture. Place a cube of Consommé on one side; press edges together, sealing completely. Repeat with remaining skins. Arrange ravioli, slightly apart, in flour-dusted 10- by 15-inch (25- by 38-cm) baking pans; cover with plastic wrap. (At this point, you may cover airtight and refrigerate for up to 8 hours; or freeze for up to 2 weeks.)

3. Bring the 2 to 2½ cups (470 to 590 ml) broth to a boil in a 1½- to 2-quart (1.4- to 1.9-liter) pan over high heat. Season to taste with salt; remove from heat and keep warm.

4. Pour water into a 5- to 6-quart (5- to 6-liter) pan to a depth of 2 to 3 inches (5 to 8 cm). Bring to a boil over high heat. Stir in ravioli, half at a time, without crowding; spoon water over ravioli or gently turn until skins become translucent and fillings liquefied (about 2 minutes). Reduce heat to low. Ladle broth into bowls. With a slotted spoon, carefully transfer ravioli. Sprinkle with cheese and chives. Makes 6 to 8 servings.

ROASTED-BONE BROTH. Cut and break into pieces about 6 pounds (2.7 kg) **poultry** and/or **meat bones** and **scrap** (cooked or raw, including poultry skin and giblets, but omitting liver; limit bare beef bones to no more than a third of total). Spread in a 12- by 17-inch (30- by 43-cm) roasting pan. Bake in a 400°F (205°C) oven until well browned (1¼ to 1½ hours).

Transfer browned pieces and drippings to a 6- to 8-quart (6- to 8-liter) pan. Using 1 to 2 tablespoons water, rinse browned bits from baking pan and add to pan. Add 8 **black peppercorns;** 2 **bay leaves;** 2 sprigs **parsley;** 2 large **onions** (about 1 lb./455 g *total*), cut into chunks; and 2 extra-large **carrots** (about 10 oz./285 g *total*), cut into chunks. Add enough **water** to almost cover ingredients.

Bring to a boil over high heat; reduce heat, cover, and simmer for 4 hours. With a slotted spoon, remove and discard big pieces. Pour broth and residue into a colander lined with a double thickness of damp cheesecloth. Let broth cool; then cover and refrigerate for at least 3 hours or up to a day.

Lift off and discard fat. Return broth to pan and cook over high heat just until melted. Measure broth. If more than 6 cups (1.4 liters), boil to reduce; if less, add water. Remove 2 to 2½ cups (470 to 590 ml) broth and reserve for cooking ravioli; use remaining broth for Consommé. If made ahead, let cool; then cover and refrigerate for up to 3 days. Makes 6 cups (1.4 liters).

CONSOMME. Combine 3½ to 4 cups (830 to 950 ml) **Roasted-bone Broth** (preceding recipe) and ½ cup (120 ml) **dry Madeira** in a wide frying pan. Bring to a boil over high heat. Cook, uncovered, until reduced to ⅔ cup/160 ml (20 to 30 minutes). Pour into a 4- by 8-inch (10- by 20-cm) loaf pan. Let cool; then cover and refrigerate for at least 1½ hours or up to a day. Cut into 32 pieces, each about ¾ by 1 inch (2 by 2.5 cm).

Per serving: 105 calories (12% fat, 75% carbohydrates, 13% protein), 1 g total fat (0.4 g saturated), 20 g carbohydrates, 4 g protein, 3 mg cholesterol, 150 mg sodium

SALADS

Lunch, brunch, buffet dinner, barbecue—there's always a time for salad. And when pasta is part of the dish, the possibilities are as varied as they are mouth-watering—satisfying without being overly filling, rich in flavor without being high in fat. The secret is in the skillful combination of a variety of pastas with fresh vegetables and fruits, poultry, seafood, lean meats, and legumes. You'll find the dressings uncommonly flavorful, too, enhancing the salad ingredients without adding unwanted calories.

◄ *Chicken & Citrus Pasta Salad (recipe on page 33)*

ZITI WITH BASIL PESTO

Preparation time: About 20 minutes

Cooking time: About 15 minutes

Chilling time: At least 30 minutes

Crunchy, sweet jicama adds texture and is the surprise ingredient in the lean pesto that coats tubular-shaped ziti for this summertime salad.

>   Basil Pesto (recipe follows)
> 10   ounces/285 g (about 3 cups) dried ziti or penne
>   2   tablespoons pine nuts (optional)
>   Basil sprigs
>   Salt and pepper
>   Freshly grated Parmesan cheese

1. Prepare Basil Pesto.

2. Bring 12 cups (2.8 liters) water to a boil in a 5- to 6-quart (5- to 6-liter) pan over medium-high heat. Stir in pasta and cook just until tender to bite (8 to 10 minutes); or cook according to package directions. Meanwhile, toast pine nuts, if desired, in a small frying pan over medium heat, shaking pan often, until golden (about 3 minutes); remove from pan and set aside.

3. Drain pasta, rinse with cold water until cool, and drain well. Transfer to a large nonmetal serving bowl. Add pesto and mix thoroughly but gently. Cover and refrigerate until cool (at least 30 minutes) or for up to 2 hours; stir occasionally.

4. Sprinkle with pine nuts, if used, and garnish with basil sprigs. Offer salt, pepper, and cheese to add to taste. Makes 6 to 8 servings.

BASIL PESTO. In a blender or food processor, combine 2 cups (80 g) lightly packed **fresh basil,** 1 cup (130 g) coarsely chopped **jicama,** ½ cup (120 ml) **low-sodium chicken broth,** ¼ cup (20 g) freshly grated **Parmesan cheese,** 3 tablespoons **olive oil,** 2 tablespoons drained **capers,** and 2 or 3 cloves **garlic.** Whirl until smooth. If made ahead, cover and refrigerate for up to an hour. Stir before using.

Per serving: 238 calories (28% fat, 59% carbohydrates, 13% protein), 8 g total fat (1 g saturated), 35 g carbohydrates, 8 g protein, 2 mg cholesterol, 126 mg sodium

CAPELLINI CHINESE STYLE

Preparation time: About 20 minutes

Cooking time: About 15 minutes

Chilling time: At least 30 minutes

Literally translated as "fine hairs," capellini are lightly dressed with a soy-based dressing and tossed with green onions and bright red bell pepper.

>   3   tablespoons seasoned rice vinegar; or 3 tablespoons distilled white vinegar and 2 teaspoons sugar
>   3   tablespoons lime juice
>   4   teaspoons Oriental sesame oil (or to taste)
>   1   tablespoon reduced-sodium soy sauce
> ¹⁄₁₆   teaspoon ground red pepper (cayenne)
>   8   ounces (230 g) dried capellini
>   ½   cup (50 g) thinly sliced green onions
>   ⅓   cup (50 g) chopped red bell pepper
>   Lime wedges

1. Combine vinegar, lime juice, oil, soy sauce, and ground red pepper in a large nonmetal serving bowl; mix until blended. Set aside.

2. Bring 8 cups (1.9 liters) water to a boil in a 4- to 5-quart (3.8- to 5-liter) pan over medium-high heat. Stir in pasta and cook just until tender to bite (about 4 minutes); or cook according to package directions. Drain, rinse with cold water until cool, and drain well.

3. Add pasta to vinegar mixture. Mix thoroughly but gently. Cover and refrigerate until cool (at least 30 minutes) or for up to 4 hours; stir occasionally.

4. Stir in onions and bell pepper just before serving. Offer lime wedges to add to taste. Makes 4 to 6 servings.

Per serving: 217 calories (18% fat, 70% carbohydrates, 12% protein), 4 g total fat (0.6 g saturated), 38 g carbohydrates, 6 g protein, 0 mg cholesterol, 305 mg sodium

SWEET & SOUR RAVIOLI SALAD

Preparation time: About 30 minutes

Cooking time: About 10 minutes

Chilling time: At least 30 minutes

Ravioli seasoned with a spicy sweet-sour dressing mingle with chunks of garden-fresh tomatoes.

- 1 package (about 9 oz./255 g) fresh low-fat or regular cheese ravioli or tortellini
- 2 pounds (905 g) pear-shaped (Roma-type) tomatoes (about 10 large)
- ½ cup (120 ml) seasoned rice vinegar; or ½ cup (120 ml) distilled white vinegar and 4 teaspoons sugar
- 2 tablespoons firmly packed brown sugar
- ½ teaspoon *each* coriander seeds, cumin seeds, and mustard seeds
- 1/16 teaspoon ground red pepper (cayenne)

  Parsley sprigs

1. Bring 12 cups (2.8 liters) water to a boil in a 5- to 6-quart (5- to 6-liter) pan over medium-high heat. Separating any ravioli that are stuck together, add pasta. Reduce heat to medium and boil gently, stirring occasionally, just until pasta is tender to bite (4 to 6 minutes); or cook according to package directions. Lift out pasta, rinse with cold water until cool, and drain well. Transfer to a large nonmetal serving bowl and set aside.

2. Bring water in pan back to a boil. Drop in tomatoes and cook for 1 minute. Drain and let cool. Peel and discard skin; cut into bite-size pieces. Set aside.

3. Combine vinegar, brown sugar, coriander seeds, cumin seeds, mustard seeds, and ground red pepper in a 1- to 1½-quart (950-ml to 1.4-liter) pan. Bring to a simmer over low heat. Cook, stirring, just until sugar is dissolved (about 1 minute).

4. Add tomatoes and vinegar mixture to pasta. Mix thoroughly but gently. Let cool briefly; then cover and refrigerate until cool (at least 30 minutes) or for up to 4 hours; stir occasionally.

5. Garnish with parsley. Makes 6 to 8 servings.

Per serving: 154 calories (15% fat, 68% carbohydrates, 17% protein), 3 g total fat (0.9 g saturated), 27 g carbohydrates, 7 g protein, 34 mg cholesterol, 485 mg sodium

FRUITED ORZO

Preparation time: About 25 minutes

Cooking time: About 15 minutes

Chilling time: At least 30 minutes

One of the reasons that pasta is so popular is that it combines easily with many different ingredients. But here's a combination that's somewhat unexpected—pasta with ripe pears and tangy cranberries. Taste the goodness of this pairing in a quick-to-make salad that complements grilled meats and poultry.

  Pear Dressing (recipe follows)
- 10 ounces/285 g (about 1⅔ cups) dried orzo or other rice-shaped pasta
- 4 large red or d'Anjou pears (about 2 lbs./ 905 g *total*)
- 3 tablespoons lemon juice
- ½ cup (65 g) roasted salted almonds, coarsely chopped

1. Prepare Pear Dressing; cover and refrigerate.

2. Bring 8 cups (1.9 liters) water to a boil in a 4- to 5-quart (3.8- to 5-liter) pan over medium-high heat. Add pasta and cook just until tender to bite (8 to 10 minutes); or cook according to package directions. Drain, rinse with cold water until cool, and drain well. Transfer to a large nonmetal bowl. Add dressing. Mix thoroughly but gently. Cover and refrigerate until cool (about 30 minutes) or for up to 3 hours; stir occasionally.

3. Slice pears thinly just before serving. Coat with lemon juice. Coarsely chop a third of the fruit and stir into pasta mixture. Spoon onto individual plates. Arrange pear slices alongside. Sprinkle with nuts. Makes 6 servings.

PEAR DRESSING. In a small nonmetal bowl, combine ¾ cup (180 ml) canned **pear nectar** or apple juice, ⅓ cup (30 g) **dried cranberries,** and ¼ cup (45 g) chopped **dried pears;** let stand, stirring occasionally, until fruit is softened (about 10 minutes). Add ½ cup (120 ml) **nonfat** or reduced-fat **sour cream,** 1 tablespoon **lemon juice,** 2 teaspoons *each* grated **lemon peel** and **ground coriander,** and 1 teaspoon **sugar** (or to taste). Mix until blended. If made ahead, cover and refrigerate for up to an hour. Stir before using.

Per serving: 414 calories (19% fat, 71% carbohydrates, 10% protein), 9 g total fat (0.8 g saturated), 77 g carbohydrates, 11 g protein, 0 mg cholesterol, 123 mg sodium

COUSCOUS TABBOULEH

Preparation time: About 15 minutes

Cooking time: About 8 minutes

Chilling time: At least 30 minutes

Redolent with mint and lemon, tabbouleh, a Middle Eastern specialty, goes together quickly and is a satisfying side dish for a summertime barbecue.

- 10 **ounces/285 g (about 1⅔ cups) dried couscous**
- 1½ **cups (55 g) firmly packed fresh mint, minced**
- 2 **tablespoons olive oil**
- ½ **cup (120 ml) lemon juice (or to taste)**
   Salt and pepper
- 6 **to 8 large butter lettuce leaves, rinsed and crisped**
- 2 **large tomatoes (about 1 lb./455 g *total*), thinly sliced**
   Mint sprigs

1. Bring 2¼ cups (530 ml) water to a boil in a 3- to 4-quart (2.8- to 3.8-liter) pan over high heat. Stir in pasta; cover, remove from heat, and let stand until liquid is absorbed (about 5 minutes). Transfer pasta to a large nonmetal bowl and let cool, fluffing occasionally with a fork.

2. Add minced mint, oil, and lemon juice to pasta. Season to taste with salt and pepper. Mix well. Cover and refrigerate until cool (at least 30 minutes) or for up to 4 hours; fluff occasionally with a fork.

3. Line a platter with lettuce leaves. Mound tabbouleh in center; arrange tomatoes around edge. Garnish with mint sprigs. Makes 6 to 8 servings.

Per serving: 210 calories (19% fat, 69% carbohydrates, 12% protein), 5 g total fat (0.6 g saturated), 37 g carbohydrates, 6 g protein, 0 mg cholesterol, 14 mg sodium

MACARONI SALAD

Pictured on facing page

Preparation time: About 30 minutes

Cooking time: About 15 minutes

Chilling time: At least 30 minutes

Tofu lends creaminess to this lightened-up salad favorite.

- **Tofu Mayonnaise (recipe follows)**
- 8 **ounces/230 g (about 2 cups) dried elbow macaroni**
- 1 **large hard-cooked egg, chopped**
- ½ **cup (60 g) thinly sliced celery**
- 1 **jar (about 2 oz./55 g) chopped pimentos, drained**
- ½ **cup (80 g) chopped dill pickles**
- ¼ **cup (25 g) thinly sliced green onions**
   Green leaf lettuce leaves, washed and crisped
   Tomato slices
   Thyme or parsley sprigs

1. Prepare Tofu Mayonnaise; cover and refrigerate.

2. Bring 8 cups (1.9 liters) water to a boil in a 4- to 5-quart (3.8- to 5-liter) pan over medium-high heat. Stir in pasta and cook just until tender to bite (8 to 10 minutes); or cook according to package directions. Drain, rinse with cold water until cool, and drain well.

3. Transfer pasta to a large nonmetal bowl. Add Tofu Mayonnaise, egg, celery, pimentos, and pickles. Mix well. Cover and refrigerate until cool (at least 30 minutes) or for up to 2 hours; stir occasionally. Just before serving, stir in onions. Arrange lettuce and tomatoes on individual plates. Top with pasta. Garnish with thyme sprigs. Makes 8 servings.

TOFU MAYONNAISE. Rinse 8 ounces (230 g) **soft tofu** in a colander. Coarsely mash tofu; let drain for 10 minutes. Transfer to a blender or food processor. Add ¼ cup (60 ml) **low-sodium chicken** or vegetable **broth,** 3 tablespoons **lemon juice,** 2 tablespoons **olive oil** or salad oil, 2 teaspoons *each* **prepared horseradish** and **sugar,** and 1 teaspoon *each* **dried thyme** and **Dijon mustard.** Whirl until smooth. Season to taste with **salt.** If made ahead, cover and refrigerate for up to an hour. Stir before using.

Per serving: 173 calories (28% fat, 58% carbohydrates, 14% protein), 5 g total fat (0.7 g saturated), 25 g carbohydrates, 6 g protein, 27 mg cholesterol, 167 mg sodium

Macaroni Salad (recipe above) ▶

CREAMY CUCUMBER & TORTELLINI SALAD

Preparation time: About 20 minutes

Cooking time: About 10 minutes

Chilling time: At least 30 minutes

Crisp cucumbers and tender fresh tortellini produce an unusual, refreshingly cool salad.

1 **package (about 9 oz./255 g) fresh cheese tortellini or ravioli**

2 **medium-size cucumbers (about 1½ lbs./ 680 g *total*)**

About ¼ teaspoon salt

2 **cups (470 ml) plain low-fat yogurt**

3 **cloves garlic, minced or pressed**

2 **tablespoons lemon juice**

1 **tablespoon minced fresh dill or 1 teaspoon dried dill weed**

2 **teaspoons olive oil (or to taste)**

8 **to 12 large butter lettuce leaves, rinsed and crisped**

1 **tablespoon minced fresh mint or 1 teaspoon dried mint**

Dill or mint sprigs

1. Bring 12 cups (2.8 liters) water to a boil in a 5- to 6-quart (5- to 6-liter) pan over medium-high heat. Stir in pasta and cook just until tender to bite (4 to 6 minutes); or cook according to package directions. Drain, rinse with cold water until cool, and drain well. Set aside.

2. Peel cucumbers, scrape out and discard seeds, and coarsely chop. In a colander, mix cucumbers with ¼ teaspoon of the salt; let drain for 15 minutes.

3. Transfer pasta to a large nonmetal bowl. Add cucumbers, yogurt, garlic, lemon juice, minced dill, and oil. Mix thoroughly but gently. Cover and refrigerate until cool (at least 30 minutes) or for up to 2 hours; stir occasionally.

4. Arrange lettuce on individual plates. Spoon pasta mixture onto lettuce and sprinkle with minced mint. Garnish with dill sprigs. Offer salt to add to taste. Makes 4 to 6 servings.

Per serving: 250 calories (21% fat, 56% carbohydrates, 23% protein), 6 g total fat (1 g saturated), 36 g carbohydrates, 14 g protein, 33 mg cholesterol, 384 mg sodium

THAI CHICKEN & CAPELLINI BUFFET

Preparation time: About 35 minutes

Cooking time: About 30 minutes

Guests can help themselves to this easily prepared buffet of chicken, noodles, and vegetables, topped with a spicy dressing. Follow with a dessert of cooling fresh pineapple.

Chili Dressing (recipe follows)

4 **chicken breast halves (2 to 2½ lbs./905 g to 1.15 kg *total*), skinned**

1 **pound (455 g) dried capellini**

2 **teaspoons Oriental sesame oil or salad oil**

1 **large European cucumber (about 1 lb./455 g), cut into thin rounds and slivered**

8 **to 12 ounces (230 to 340 g) bean sprouts, rinsed and drained**

¾ **cup (75 g) thinly sliced green onions**

¾ **cup (30 g) chopped cilantro**

½ **cup (20 g) chopped fresh basil**

¾ **cup (110 g) finely chopped salted roasted peanuts**

Lemon wedges (optional)

1. Prepare Chili Dressing; cover and refrigerate.

2. Bring 16 cups (3.8 liters) water to a boil in a 6- to 8-quart (6- to 8-liter) pan over high heat. Add chicken and return to a boil. Cover pan tightly, remove from heat, and let stand until meat in thickest part is no longer pink; cut to test (about 20 minutes). If not done, return chicken to water, cover, and let stand, checking for doneness at 2- or 3-minute intervals. Lift out chicken, reserving water, and let cool. Meanwhile, return water to a boil over medium-high heat. Stir in pasta and cook just until tender to bite (about 4 minutes); or cook according to package directions. Drain, rinse with cold water until cool, and drain well.

3. Sprinkle pasta with oil. Loosely coil small handfuls of pasta; set on a rimmed platter, stacking if necessary. Drizzle with about 1 cup (240 ml) of the dressing. Tear chicken into shreds; discard bones. Arrange chicken, cucumber, sprouts, and onions separately around pasta. Drizzle with remaining dressing (or to taste). Place cilantro, basil, nuts, and, if desired, lemon in small bowls and offer to add to taste. Makes 6 servings.

CHILI DRESSING. In a small nonmetal bowl, combine ¾ cup (180 ml) **rice vinegar** or white wine vinegar, ½ cup (120 ml) **reduced-sodium soy sauce,** 3 tablespoons **sugar,** 2 tablespoons *each* minced **fresh ginger** and **Oriental sesame oil,** 1 to 2 teaspoons **crushed red pepper flakes,** and 2 cloves **garlic,** minced or pressed. Mix until blended. If made ahead, cover and refrigerate for up to 4 hours. Stir before using. Makes about 1⅔ cups (400 ml).

Per serving: 638 calories (25% fat, 48% carbohydrates, 27% protein), 18 g total fat (3 g saturated), 77 g carbohydrates, 44 g protein, 64 mg cholesterol, 963 mg sodium

CHICKEN & CITRUS PASTA SALAD

Pictured on page 26

Preparation time: About 1 hour

Cooking time: About 25 minutes

Chilling time: At least 30 minutes

A basil-citrus pasta salad made with corkscrew-shaped rotini accompanies naturally lean chicken breasts and sliced oranges.

- 2 **large oranges (about 1 lb./455 g** *total*)
  Citrus Pasta Salad (recipe follows)
  Orange Cream (recipe follows)
- ¼ **cup (80 g) orange marmalade**
- 1 **teaspoon prepared horseradish**
- 6 **skinless, boneless chicken breast halves (about 1½ lbs./680 g** *total*)
- 2 **large blood oranges (about 10 oz./285 g** *total*) **or 1 small pink grapefruit (about 6 oz./170 g)**
- 2 **medium-size avocados (about 1 lb./455 g** *total*), **optional**
- 2 **tablespoons lemon juice (optional)**
  Basil sprigs
  Finely shredded orange peel

1. Grate 4 teaspoons peel from oranges. Prepare Citrus Pasta Salad and Orange Cream, using grated peel; cover and refrigerate.

2. Mix marmalade and horseradish in a large bowl. Add chicken and stir to coat. Place chicken in a lightly oiled 10- by 15-inch (25- by 38-cm) baking pan. Bake in a 450°F (230°C) oven until meat in thickest part is no longer pink; cut to test (12 to 15 minutes). Let cool. Meanwhile, cut peel and white membrane from oranges and blood oranges; slice fruit crosswise into rounds ¼ inch (6 mm) thick. (For grapefruit, cut segments from membrane; discard membrane.)

3. Arrange pasta salad and chicken on a platter. Place fruit around edge. If desired, pit, peel, and slice avocados; coat with lemon juice and place on platter. Garnish with basil sprigs and shredded orange peel. Offer Orange Cream to add to taste. Makes 6 servings.

CITRUS PASTA SALAD. Bring 12 cups (2.8 liters) **water** to a boil in a 5- to 6-quart (5- to 6-liter) pan over medium-high heat. Stir in 12 ounces/340 g (about 5 cups) **dried rotini** or other corkscrew-shaped pasta. Cook just until tender to bite (8 to 10 minutes); or cook according to package directions. Drain, rinse with cold water until cool, and drain well.

In a large nonmetal bowl, combine 1 tablespoon grated **orange peel;** ¾ cup (180 ml) **orange juice;** 1 small **orange** (about 4 oz./115 g), peeled and coarsely chopped; 3 tablespoons **white wine vinegar** or distilled white vinegar; 3 tablespoons chopped **fresh basil;** 1 tablespoon *each* **honey** and **Dijon mustard;** 1½ teaspoons **ground cumin;** and 1 **fresh jalapeño chile,** seeded and finely chopped. Mix until blended. Add pasta and mix thoroughly but gently. Cover and refrigerate until cool (at least 30 minutes) or for up to 4 hours; stir occasionally. Just before serving, stir in ¼ cup (15 g) chopped **parsley** and 2 or 3 cloves **garlic,** minced or pressed.

Per serving without cream: 463 calories (7% fat, 60% carbohydrates, 33% protein), 4 g total fat (0.7 g saturated), 70 g carbohydrates, 38 g protein, 74 mg cholesterol, 173 mg sodium

ORANGE CREAM. In a small nonmetal bowl, combine 1 cup (240 ml) **nonfat** or reduced-fat **sour cream,** 3 tablespoons **orange marmalade,** 2 teaspoons **prepared horseradish,** and 1 teaspoon grated **orange peel.** Mix until blended. Season to taste with **ground white pepper.** If made ahead, cover and refrigerate for up to a day. Stir before serving. Makes about 1¼ cups (300 ml).

Per tablespoon: 16 calories (0% fat, 78% carbohydrates, 22% protein), 0 g total fat (0 g saturated), 3 g carbohydrates, 0.8 g protein, 0 mg cholesterol, 10 mg sodium

LITCHI, PENNE & CHICKEN SALAD

Preparation time: About 20 minutes

Cooking time: About 20 minutes

Sweet litchis bring refreshing flavor to a chicken and pasta salad bathed in a lemony yogurt dressing. Look for litchis in Asian markets or in the Asian section of your supermarket.

      5 ounces/140 g (about 1½ cups) dried penne
      1 can (about 11 oz./310 g) litchis
      ¾ cup (180 ml) plain low-fat or nonfat yogurt
      ¾ teaspoon grated lemon peel
      4 teaspoons lemon juice
   1½ teaspoons dried thyme
      2 cups (280 g) bite-size pieces cooked chicken
      ½ cup (60 g) finely diced celery
      8 large butter lettuce leaves, rinsed and crisped
      ⅓ cup (35 g) chopped green onions
         Salt and pepper

1. Bring 8 cups (1.9 liters) water to a boil in a 4- to 5-quart (3.8- to 5-liter) pan over medium-high heat. Stir in pasta and cook just until tender to bite (8 to 10 minutes); or cook according to package directions. Drain, rinse with cold water until cool, and drain well.

2. Drain litchis, reserving ⅓ cup (80 ml) of the syrup; set fruit aside. In a large nonmetal bowl, mix reserved ⅓ cup (80 ml) litchi syrup, yogurt, lemon peel, lemon juice, and thyme. Add pasta, chicken, and celery. Mix thoroughly but gently. (At this point, you may cover pasta mixture and fruit separately and refrigerate for up to 4 hours; stir pasta occasionally.)

3. Arrange lettuce on individual plates. Top with pasta mixture and litchis. Sprinkle with onions. Offer salt and pepper to add to taste. Makes 4 servings.

Per serving: 358 calories (17% fat, 52% carbohydrates, 31% protein), 7 g total fat (2 g saturated), 47 g carbohydrates, 28 g protein, 65 mg cholesterol, 136 mg sodium

WATERCRESS, PENNE & TURKEY SALAD

Preparation time: About 25 minutes

Cooking time: About 15 minutes

Chilling time: At least 30 minutes

Peppery watercress contributes sparkling color to this salad of turkey and penne ("quill pens").

      ⅔ pound (300 g) watercress, stems trimmed, rinsed and crisped
         Watercress Dressing (recipe follows)
   10 ounces/285 g (about 3 cups) dried penne
      1 to 1¼ pounds (455 to 565 g) cooked turkey breast, cut into thin strips

1. Reserve ¾ cup (25 g) of the watercress for dressing. Prepare Watercress Dressing; cover and refrigerate.

2. Bring 12 cups (2.8 liters) water to a boil in a 5- to 6-quart (5- to 6-liter) pan over medium-high heat. Stir in pasta and cook just until tender to bite (8 to 10 minutes); or cook according to package directions. Drain, rinse with cold water until cool, and drain well.

3. Transfer pasta to a large nonmetal serving bowl. Add remaining watercress and about 1 cup (240 ml) of the dressing. Mix thoroughly but gently. Cover and refrigerate until cool (at least 30 minutes) or for up to 2 hours; stir occasionally.

4. Mound turkey on pasta mixture. Offer remaining dressing to add to taste. Makes 6 servings.

Per serving: 321 calories (4% fat, 52% carbohydrates, 44% protein), 1 g total fat (0.3 g saturated), 40 g carbohydrates, 34 g protein, 71 mg cholesterol, 221 mg sodium

WATERCRESS DRESSING. In a blender or food processor, combine reserved ¾ cup (25 g) **watercress,** ¾ cup (180 ml) **plain nonfat** or low-fat **yogurt,** ¾ cup (180 ml) **nonfat** or reduced-calorie **mayonnaise,** 1 tablespoon **lemon juice,** ½ teaspoon **dried basil,** and 1 clove **garlic.** Whirl until smooth. Season to taste with **sugar** and **fish sauce** (*nam pla* or *nuoc mam*) or reduced-sodium soy sauce. Whirl until blended. If made ahead, cover and refrigerate for up to an hour. Stir before using. Makes 1⅔ cups (400 ml).

Per tablespoon: 9 calories (1% fat, 78% carbohydrates, 21% protein), 0 g total fat (0 g saturated), 2 g carbohydrates, 0.4 g protein, 0.1 mg cholesterol, 54 mg sodium

◄ *Smoked Salmon Pasta Salad (recipe on page 36)*

SMOKED SALMON PASTA SALAD

Pictured on page 34

Preparation time: About 15 minutes

Cooking time: About 15 minutes

This elegant salad features smoked salmon and fresh dill.

- 8 ounces/230 g (about 3 cups) dried radiatorre or rotini
- ¼ cup (60 ml) seasoned rice vinegar; or ¼ cup (60 ml) distilled white vinegar and 2 teaspoons sugar
- 1 tablespoon chopped fresh dill or ½ teaspoon dried dill weed
- 1 tablespoon olive oil
- 8 cups (440 g) bite-size pieces green leaf lettuce leaves
- ¼ cup (30 g) thinly sliced red onion
- 2 to 4 ounces (55 to 115 g) sliced smoked salmon or lox, cut into bite-size pieces

  Dill sprigs

  Freshly grated Parmesan cheese

1. Bring 8 cups (1.9 liters) water to a boil in a 4- to 5-quart (3.8- to 5-liter) pan over medium-high heat. Stir in pasta and cook just until tender to bite (8 to 10 minutes); or cook according to package directions. Drain, rinse with cold water until cool, and drain well.

2. Combine vinegar, chopped dill, and oil in a large nonmetal serving bowl. Mix until blended. Add pasta, lettuce, and onion. Mix thoroughly but gently. Stir in salmon. Garnish with dill sprigs. Offer cheese to add to taste. Makes 6 servings.

Per serving: 194 calories (16% fat, 67% carbohydrates, 17% protein), 4 g total fat (0.5 g saturated), 32 g carbohydrates, 8 g protein, 3 mg cholesterol, 316 mg sodium

SHRIMP & ORZO WITH PESTO DRESSING

Preparation time: About 25 minutes

Cooking time: About 10 minutes

Fresh basil and cilantro lend flavor and color to the creamy dressing for this cooling pasta and shrimp salad, nestled in a bed of crisp shredded lettuce.

  Pesto Dressing (recipe follows)
- 6 cups (1.4 liters) low-sodium chicken broth
- 8 ounces/230 g (about 1⅓ cups) dried orzo or other rice-shaped pasta
- 1 pound (455 g) tiny cooked shrimp
- 1 cup (100 g) chopped green onions
- 1 tablespoon grated lemon peel
- ½ cup (120 ml) lemon juice
- 1 small head iceberg lettuce (about 1 lb./455 g), rinsed and crisped
- 3 cups (425 g) tiny cherry tomatoes

1. Prepare Pesto Dressing; cover and refrigerate.

2. Bring broth to a boil in a 4- to 5-quart (3.8- to 5-liter) pan over medium-high heat. Stir in pasta and cook just until barely tender to bite (about 5 minutes). Drain well, reserving liquid for other uses. Let cool completely.

3. Transfer pasta to a large bowl. Add shrimp, onions, lemon peel, and lemon juice. Mix thoroughly but gently.

4. Shred lettuce and place in a shallow serving bowl. Spoon pasta mixture into bowl. Arrange tomatoes around edge of bowl. Offer dressing to add to taste. Makes 5 or 6 servings.

Per serving without dressing: 280 calories (11% fat, 54% carbohydrates, 35% protein), 3 g total fat (0.7 g saturated), 37 g carbohydrates, 25 g protein, 148 mg cholesterol, 244 mg sodium

PESTO DRESSING. In a blender or food processor, combine ½ cup (20 g) *each* chopped **fresh basil** and chopped **cilantro,** 1 cup (240 ml) **plain nonfat yogurt,** and 1 tablespoon **white wine vinegar.** Whirl until smooth. If made ahead, cover and refrigerate for up to 4 hours. Stir before serving. Makes about 1¼ cups (300 ml).

Per tablespoon: 8 calories (4% fat, 60% carbohydrates, 36% protein), 0 g total fat (0 g saturated), 1 g carbohydrates, 0.7 g protein, 0.2 mg cholesterol, 9 mg sodium

CURRIED SHRIMP & SHELL SALAD

Preparation time: About 25 minutes

Cooking time: About 15 minutes

Chilling time: At least 30 minutes

Make this salad ahead of time to enjoy on a warm summer day, along with fresh fruit and crisp toast.

> **Curry Dressing (recipe follows)**
> 2 ounces/55 g (about ½ cup) dried small shell-shaped pasta
> 12 ounces (340 g) tiny cooked shrimp
> 1 cup (145 g) coarsely chopped cucumber
> 3 tablespoons dried tomatoes packed in oil, drained well and coarsely chopped
> **Salt**
> 4 to 8 large butter lettuce leaves, rinsed and crisped
> **Lemon wedges**

1. Prepare Curry Dressing; cover and refrigerate.

2. Bring 4 cups (950 ml) water to a boil in a 3- to 4-quart (2.8- to 3.8-liter) pan over medium-high heat. Stir in pasta and cook just until tender to bite (8 to 10 minutes); or cook according to package directions. Drain, rinse with cold water until cool, and drain well.

3. Transfer pasta to a large nonmetal bowl. Add shrimp, cucumber, tomatoes, and dressing. Mix thoroughly but gently. Season to taste with salt. Cover and refrigerate until cool (at least 30 minutes) or for up to 4 hours; stir occasionally.

4. Arrange lettuce on individual plates. Spoon pasta mixture onto lettuce. Offer lemon to add to taste. Makes 4 servings.

CURRY DRESSING. In a small nonmetal bowl, combine ¼ cup (60 ml) **nonfat** or reduced-calorie **mayonnaise,** 1 tablespoon **Dijon mustard,** ½ teaspoon grated **lemon peel,** 1 tablespoon **lemon juice,** 1 teaspoon *each* **dried dill weed** and **honey,** ½ teaspoon **curry powder,** and ¼ teaspoon **pepper.** Mix until blended. If made ahead, cover and refrigerate for up to an hour. Stir before using.

Per serving: 227 calories (29% fat, 34% carbohydrates, 37% protein), 7 g total fat (1 g saturated), 19 g carbohydrates, 21 g protein, 166 mg cholesterol, 417 mg sodium

BEEF & BOW-TIE SALAD

Preparation time: About 30 minutes

Marinating time: At least 30 minutes

Cooking time: About 20 minutes

Chilling time: At least 30 minutes

Mild butter lettuce in a creamy tofu-enriched blue cheese dressing cradles a hearty salad of marinated beef and bow-tie pasta.

> 1 pound (455 g) lean boneless top sirloin steak (about 1 inch/2.5 cm thick), trimmed of fat
> 2 tablespoons dry sherry
> **Blue Cheese Dressing (recipe follows)**
> 6 to 8 ounces/170 to 230 g (3 to 4 cups) dried farfalle (about 1½-inch/3.5-cm size)
> ¼ cup (60 ml) red wine vinegar
> 1 tablespoon olive oil or salad oil
> 1 tablespoon chopped fresh thyme or 1 teaspoon dried thyme
> 1 teaspoon sugar
> **Salt and pepper**
> 8 cups (440 g) bite-size pieces butter lettuce leaves
> **Thyme sprigs**

1. Slice steak across grain into strips about ⅛ inch (3 mm) thick and 3 inches (8 cm) long. Place meat and sherry in a large heavy-duty resealable plastic bag or nonmetal bowl. Seal bag and rotate to coat meat (or stir meat in bowl and cover airtight). Refrigerate for at least 30 minutes or up to a day, turning (or stirring) occasionally.

2. Prepare Blue Cheese Dressing; cover and refrigerate.

3. Bring 8 cups (1.9 liters) water to a boil in a 4- to 5-quart (3.8- to 5-liter) pan over medium-high heat. Stir in pasta and cook just until tender to bite (8 to 10 minutes); or cook according to package directions. Drain, rinse with cold water until cool, and drain well.

4. Combine vinegar, 2 teaspoons of the oil, chopped thyme, and sugar in a large nonmetal bowl. Stir until blended. Add pasta and mix thoroughly but gently. Cover and refrigerate until cool (at least 30 minutes) or for up to 2 hours; stir occasionally. Meanwhile, heat remaining 1 teaspoon oil in a wide nonstick frying pan over medium-high heat. Add steak and its juices and cook, stirring, until browned and done to your liking; cut to test (3 to 5 minutes). Transfer to a large nonmetal bowl and let cool. Season to taste with salt and pepper.

5. Combine lettuce and dressing in a large serving bowl; turn to coat. Add beef to pasta mixture and stir gently. Spoon onto greens. Garnish with thyme sprigs. Makes 4 to 6 servings.

BLUE CHEESE DRESSING. In a blender or food processor, combine 4 ounces (115 g) **low-fat (1%)** or soft **tofu,** rinsed and drained; ¼ cup (60 ml) **low-fat buttermilk;** 1 tablespoon **white wine vinegar;** 2 teaspoons *each* **sugar** and **olive oil;** 1 teaspoon **Dijon mustard;** and 1 clove **garlic.** Whirl until smooth. Season to taste with **salt** and **pepper.** Gently stir in ¼ cup (35 g) crumbled **blue-veined cheese.** (At this point, you may cover and refrigerate for up to an hour.) Stir in 1 tablespoon chopped **green onion** before using.

Per serving: 376 calories (29% fat, 40% carbohydrates, 31% protein), 12 g total fat (3 g saturated), 37 g carbohydrates, 29 g protein, 61 mg cholesterol, 216 mg sodium

STEAK, COUSCOUS & GREENS WITH RASPBERRIES

Pictured on facing page

Preparation time: About 1 hour

Marinating time: At least 30 minutes

Cooking time: About 15 minutes

Chilling time: At least 30 minutes

When raspberries are in season, enjoy this quickly cooked beef and pasta salad. Fresh raspberries adorn the salad, and raspberry flavor infuses the beef, pasta, and lettuce.

1	pound (455 g) lean boneless top sirloin steak (about 1 inch/2.5 cm thick), trimmed of fat
½	cup (120 ml) dry red wine
5	tablespoons (75 ml) raspberry vinegar or red wine vinegar
¼	cup (25 g) chopped green onions
2	tablespoons reduced-sodium soy sauce
1	tablespoon sugar
2	teaspoons chopped fresh tarragon or ½ teaspoon dried tarragon
1	tablespoon raspberry or apple jelly
¾	cup (180 ml) low-sodium chicken broth
⅔	cup (160 ml) low-fat milk
¼	teaspoon ground coriander
6½	ounces/185 g (about 1 cup) dried couscous
1	tablespoon olive oil
8	cups (440 g) bite-size pieces red leaf lettuce leaves
2	cups (245 g) raspberries
	Tarragon sprigs (optional)

1. Slice steak across grain into strips about ⅛ inch (3 mm) thick and 3 inches (8 cm) long. Place meat, wine, 1 tablespoon of the vinegar, 2 tablespoons of the onions, soy sauce, 2 teaspoons of the sugar, and chopped tarragon in a large heavy-duty resealable plastic bag or large nonmetal bowl. Seal bag and rotate to coat meat (or stir meat in bowl and cover airtight). Refrigerate for at least 30 minutes or up to a day, turning (or stirring) occasionally.

2. Cook jelly in a 2- to 3-quart (1.9- to 2.8-liter) pan over low heat, stirring, until melted. Add broth, milk, and coriander; increase heat to medium-high and bring to a gentle boil. Stir in couscous. Cover, remove from heat, and let stand until liquid is absorbed (about 5 minutes).

3. Transfer couscous mixture to a large nonmetal bowl; let cool briefly, fluffing occasionally with a fork. Cover and refrigerate until cool (at least 30 minutes) or for up to 2 hours, fluffing occasionally. Meanwhile, heat 1 teaspoon of the oil in a wide nonstick frying pan over medium-high heat. Add meat and its juices and cook, stirring, until browned and done to your liking; cut to test (3 to 5 minutes). Transfer to a large nonmetal bowl and let cool.

4. Combine remaining 2 teaspoons oil, remaining 4 tablespoons vinegar, and remaining 1 teaspoon sugar in a large nonmetal bowl. Mix until blended. Add lettuce and turn to coat. Arrange lettuce on individual plates. Stir remaining 2 tablespoons onions into couscous mixture. Spoon onto lettuce, top with meat, and sprinkle with raspberries. Garnish with tarragon sprigs, if desired. Makes 4 servings.

Per serving: 457 calories (20% fat, 50% carbohydrates, 30% protein), 10 g total fat (3 g saturated), 55 g carbohydrates, 34 g protein, 71 mg cholesterol, 262 mg sodium

*Steak, Couscous & Greens with Raspberries ▶
(recipe above left)*

LENTIL & PAPPARDELLE SALAD

Preparation time: About 20 minutes

Cooking time: About 40 minutes

Chilling time: At least 30 minutes

Lentils and pasta mingle in this unusual side-dish salad, enhanced by a minty, tart-sweet dressing.

- 2 cups (470 ml) beef broth
- 6 ounces/170 g (about 1 cup) lentils, rinsed and drained
- 1 teaspoon dried oregano
- 6 ounces (170 g) dried pappardelle or extra-wide egg noodles
- ⅓ cup (80 ml) lemon juice
- 3 tablespoons chopped fresh mint or 1 teaspoon dried mint
- 2 tablespoons olive oil
- 1 teaspoon honey (or to taste)
- 6 cups (330 g) shredded red leaf lettuce leaves
- 1 or 2 cloves garlic, minced or pressed
- ⅔ cup (85 g) crumbled feta cheese (or to taste)
  Mint sprigs

1. Bring broth to a boil in a 1½- to 2-quart (1.4- to 1.9-liter) pan over high heat. Add lentils and oregano; reduce heat, cover, and simmer just until lentils are tender to bite (20 to 30 minutes). Drain, if necessary. Transfer to a large nonmetal bowl and let cool. Meanwhile, bring 8 cups (1.9 liters) water to a boil in a 4- to 5-quart (3.8- to 5-liter) pan over medium-high heat. Stir in pasta and cook just until tender to bite (8 to 10 minutes); or cook according to package directions. Drain, rinse with cold water until cool, and drain well.

2. Add pasta, lemon juice, chopped mint, oil, and honey to lentils. Mix thoroughly but gently. Cover and refrigerate until cool (at least 30 minutes) or for up to 4 hours; stir occasionally.

3. Arrange lettuce on a platter. Stir garlic into pasta mixture and spoon onto lettuce. Sprinkle with cheese. Garnish with mint sprigs. Makes 6 to 8 servings.

Per serving: 274 calories (27% fat, 53% carbohydrates, 20% protein), 8 g total fat (3 g saturated), 37 g carbohydrates, 14 g protein, 34 mg cholesterol, 386 mg sodium

PORK & ROTINI SALAD WITH ORANGES

Preparation time: About 30 minutes

Cooking time: About 10 minutes

Chilling time: At least 30 minutes

Serve this salad on a bed of orange slices and spinach.

- 8 ounces/230 g (about 3½ cups) dried rotini or other corkscrew-shaped pasta
- 1 teaspoon salad oil
- 1 pound (455 g) pork tenderloin or boned pork loin, trimmed of fat, sliced into thin strips ½ inch (1 cm) wide
- 1 tablespoon minced garlic
- 1 teaspoon *each* chili powder and dried oregano
- ¾ cup (180 ml) lime juice
- 3 tablespoons sugar
- 1 teaspoon reduced-sodium soy sauce
- ⅓ cup (15 g) chopped cilantro
- 6 large oranges (about 3½ lbs./1.6 kg *total*)
  About 40 large spinach leaves, coarse stems removed, rinsed and crisped

1. Bring 8 cups (1.9 liters) water to a boil in a 4- to 5-quart (3.8- to 5-liter) pan over medium-high heat. Stir in pasta and cook just until tender to bite (8 to 10 minutes); or cook according to package directions. Drain, rinse with cold water until cool, and drain well; set aside.

2. Heat oil in a wide nonstick frying pan over medium-high heat. Add pork, garlic, chili powder, and oregano. Cook, stirring, until pork is no longer pink in center; cut to test (about 5 minutes). Remove pan from heat and add lime juice, sugar, and soy sauce; stir to loosen browned bits. Transfer to a large nonmetal bowl and let cool briefly. Add pasta and cilantro. Mix thoroughly but gently. Cover and refrigerate until cool (at least 30 minutes) or for up to 2 hours; stir occasionally.

3. Cut peel and white membrane from oranges; thinly slice fruit crosswise. Arrange spinach on individual plates. Top with orange slices and pasta mixture. Makes 6 servings.

Per serving: 362 calories (11% fat, 64% carbohydrates, 25% protein), 5 g total fat (1 g saturated), 59 g carbohydrates, 23 g protein, 49 mg cholesterol, 99 mg sodium

Gingered Pork & Ziti Salad

Preparation time: About 30 minutes

Cooking time: About 15 minutes

Chilling time: At least 30 minutes

A mango and ginger dressing bastes roasted pork and tubular ziti in an appetizing, no-fuss salad.

- 6 ounces/170 g (about 2 cups) dried ziti or penne
- ⅔ cup (160 ml) mango or pear nectar
- 1 tablespoon minced fresh ginger
- 2 teaspoons olive oil
- 1 or 2 cloves garlic, minced or pressed
- 1 teaspoon Oriental sesame oil
- 1½ cups (210 g) roasted or Chinese-style barbecued pork, cut into thin ½-inch (1-cm) pieces
- ⅓ cup (50 g) chopped red bell pepper
- 4 to 8 red leaf lettuce leaves, rinsed and crisped
- ¼ cup (25 g) thinly sliced green onions
- 4 whole green onions (optional)
- Salt and pepper

1. Bring 8 cups (1.9 liters) water to a boil in a 4- to 5-quart (3.8- to 5-liter) pan over medium-high heat. Stir in pasta and cook just until tender to bite (8 to 10 minutes); or cook according to package directions. Drain, rinse with cold water until cool, and drain well.

2. Combine mango nectar, ginger, olive oil, garlic, and sesame oil in a large nonmetal bowl. Mix until blended. Add pasta, pork, and bell pepper. Mix thoroughly but gently. Cover and refrigerate until cool (at least 30 minutes) or for up to 3 hours; stir occasionally.

3. Arrange lettuce on individual plates. Stir sliced onions into pasta mixture and spoon onto lettuce. Garnish with whole onions, if desired. Offer salt and pepper to add to taste. Makes 4 servings.

Per serving: 346 calories (26% fat, 46% carbohydrates, 28% protein), 10 g total fat (3 g saturated), 40 g carbohydrates, 24 g protein, 50 mg cholesterol, 51 mg sodium

Cool Beans & Bows

Preparation time: About 15 minutes

Cooking time: About 15 minutes

Chilling time: At least 30 minutes

Combining pasta with beans, creates a complete protein.

- 4 ounces/115 g (about 2 cups) dried farfalle (about 1½-inch/3.5-cm size)
- ½ cup (120 ml) seasoned rice vinegar; or ½ cup (120 ml) distilled white vinegar and 4 teaspoons sugar
- ¼ cup (15 g) minced parsley
- 1 tablespoon *each* olive oil, water, and honey
- ¼ teaspoon chili oil
- 1 can (about 15 oz./425 g) kidney beans or 2 cups cooked (about 1 cup/185 g dried) kidney beans, drained and rinsed
- 1 can (about 15 oz./425 g) black beans or 2 cups cooked (about 1 cup/200 g dried) black beans, drained and rinsed
- 1 large pear-shaped (Roma-type) tomato (about 4 oz./115 g), diced
- ¼ cup (25 g) thinly sliced green onions

1. Bring 8 cups (1.9 liters) water to a boil in a 4- to 5-quart (3.8- to 5-liter) pan over medium-high heat. Stir in pasta and cook just until tender to bite (8 to 10 minutes); or cook according to package directions. Drain, rinse with cold water until cool, and drain well.

2. Combine vinegar, parsley, olive oil, water, honey, and chili oil in a large nonmetal bowl. Mix well. Add kidney and black beans, pasta, and tomato. Mix thoroughly but gently. Cover and refrigerate until cool (at least 30 minutes) or for up to 4 hours; stir occasionally.

3. Stir onions into pasta mixture just before serving. Transfer to a large serving bowl. Makes 4 to 6 servings.

Per serving: 257 calories (14% fat, 69% carbohydrates, 17% protein), 4 g total fat (0.5 g saturated), 44 g carbohydrates, 11 g protein, 0 mg cholesterol, 724 mg sodium

POULTRY & SEAFOOD

When pasta is combined with naturally lean poultry or seafood, you have the makings of a nutritious, low-fat entrée. And when tossed with an imaginative sauce, you have a dish that will please the most discriminating palate—and satisfy the most ravenous appetite. From international specialties, such as Chicken & Shrimp Pansit, to lightened-up family favorites, such as Spaghetti with Turkey Meatballs, you're sure to find the perfect recipe here for every taste and occasion.

◄ *Stuffed Chicken Legs with Capellini*
   (recipe on page 44)

STUFFED CHICKEN LEGS WITH CAPELLINI

Pictured on page 42

Preparation time: About 25 minutes

Cooking time: About 1 hour

While you grill the vegetables and chicken for this recipe, the capellini cooks quickly on the stovetop.

- ½ **cup (20 g)** *each* **cilantro leaves and fresh basil**
- ½ **cup (40 g) freshly grated Parmesan cheese**
- 3 **whole chicken legs (about 1½ lbs./680 g** *total***)**
- 3 **large red bell peppers (about 1½ lbs./680 g** *total***)**
- 4 **slices bacon**
- 12 **ounces (340 g) dried capellini**
- ½ **cup (120 ml) seasoned rice vinegar; or ½ cup (120 ml) distilled white vinegar and 4 teaspoons sugar**
- ¼ **cup (30 g) capers, drained**
- 1 **tablespoon grated lemon peel**
  Finely shredded lemon peel
  Cilantro sprigs
  Salt and pepper

1. Combine cilantro leaves, basil, and cheese in a food processor or blender. Whirl until minced.

2. Cut a slit just through skin at joint on outside of each chicken leg. Slide your fingers between skin and meat to separate, leaving skin in place. Tuck cilantro mixture under skin, spreading evenly. Set aside.

3. Place bell peppers on a lightly greased grill 4 to 6 inches (10 to 15 cm) above a solid bed of hot coals. Grill, turning as needed, until charred all over (about 10 minutes). Cover with foil and let cool. Pull off and discard skin, stems, and seeds. Cut into strips and set aside.

4. Lay chicken on grill when coals have cooled down to medium heat and cook, turning as needed, until meat near thighbone is no longer pink; cut to test (about 40 minutes). Meanwhile, cook bacon in a wide nonstick frying pan over medium heat until crisp (about 5 minutes). Lift out, drain well, and crumble; set aside. Discard all but 2 teaspoons of the drippings; set pan with drippings aside.

5. Bring 12 cups (2.8 liters) water to a boil in a 5- to 6-quart (5- to 6-liter) pan over medium-high heat. Stir in pasta and cook just until tender to bite (about 4 minutes); or cook according to package directions. Drain well and keep warm.

6. Add vinegar, capers, and grated lemon peel to pan with drippings. Bring just to a boil over medium heat. Add pasta and bacon. Cook, stirring, just until warm. Transfer to a platter. Cut chicken legs apart. Place chicken and bell peppers on platter. Garnish with shredded lemon peel and cilantro sprigs. Offer salt and pepper to add to taste. Makes 6 servings.

Per serving: 457 calories (29% fat, 46% carbohydrates, 25% protein), 15 g total fat (5 g saturated), 52 g carbohydrates, 28 g protein, 64 mg cholesterol, 858 mg sodium

CHICKEN VERMICELLI CARBONARA

Preparation time: About 25 minutes

Cooking time: About 30 minutes

Enjoy this low-fat version of the Italian pasta classic.

- 1 **large onion (about 8 oz./230 g), chopped**
- ½ **teaspoon fennel seeds**
- 1¾ **cups (420 ml) low-sodium chicken broth**
- 12 **to 14 ounces (340 to 400 g) boneless, skinless chicken thighs, trimmed of fat, cut into ½-inch (1-cm) chunks**
- 1 **cup (60 g) finely chopped parsley**
- 3 **large egg whites (about 6 tablespoons/90 ml)**
- 1 **large egg**
- 12 **to 16 ounces (340 to 455 g) dried vermicelli**
- 1½ **cups (about 6 oz./170 g) finely shredded Parmesan cheese**
  Salt and pepper

1. Combine onion, fennel seeds, and 1 cup (240 ml) of the broth in a wide nonstick frying pan. Bring to a boil over high heat; cook, stirring occasionally, until liquid has evaporated and onion begins to brown (about 10 minutes). To deglaze pan, add 2 tablespoons water, stirring to loosen browned bits. Continue to cook, stirring often, until liquid has evaporated and onion begins to brown again. Repeat deglazing step, adding 2 tablespoons more water each time, until onion is golden brown.

2. Add chicken and 2 tablespoons more water to pan, stirring to loosen browned bits. Cook, stirring often, until drippings begin to brown. Repeat deglazing step, adding 2 tablespoons more water. When pan is dry, add remaining ¾ cup (180 ml) broth and bring to a boil. Stir in parsley. Remove from heat and keep warm.

3. Beat eggs whites and whole egg in a small bowl until well blended; set aside.

4. Bring 16 cups (3.8 liters) water to a boil in a 6- to 8-quart (6- to 8-liter) pan over medium-high heat. Stir in pasta and cook just until tender to bite (8 to 10 minutes); or cook according to package directions. Drain well. Quickly add hot pasta to chicken, pour on egg mixture, and lift with 2 forks to mix, gradually adding 1 cup (115 g) of the cheese. Transfer to a platter and continue to mix until most of the broth is absorbed. Offer salt, pepper, and remaining ½ cup (55 g) cheese to add to taste. Makes 6 to 8 servings.

Per serving: 430 calories (25% fat, 45% carbohydrates, 30% protein), 12 g total fat (6 g saturated), 48 g carbohydrates, 32 g protein, 96 mg cholesterol, 555 mg sodium

ROAST TURKEY WITH APPLE ORZO

Pictured on page 47

Preparation time: About 20 minutes

Cooking time: About 2¼ hours

Turkey and cranberries have long been traditional partners. Here they're combined in an entirely new way.

- 2 tablespoons chopped pecans
- 1 boned turkey breast half (3 to 3½ lbs./ 1.35 to 1.6 kg), trimmed of fat
- ⅓ cup (100 g) apple jelly
- 1 tablespoon raspberry vinegar or red wine vinegar
- ¼ teaspoon ground sage
- 2 cups (470 ml) apple juice
  About 2¾ cups (650 ml) low-sodium chicken broth
- 10 ounces/285 g (about 1⅔ cups) dried orzo or other rice-shaped pasta
- ½ cup (45 g) dried cranberries or raisins

- ¼ teaspoon ground coriander
- 1 tablespoon cornstarch mixed with 3 tablespoons cold water
- ⅓ cup (20 g) chopped parsley or green onions
  Sage sprigs
  Salt and pepper

1. Toast nuts in a small frying pan over medium heat, shaking pan often, until golden (about 4 minutes). Remove from pan and set aside.

2. Place turkey skin side up. Fold narrow end under breast; pull skin to cover as much breast as possible. Tie snugly lengthwise and crosswise with cotton string at 1-inch (2.5-cm) intervals. Place in a nonstick or lightly oiled square 8-inch (20-cm) pan.

3. Combine jelly, vinegar, and ground sage in a 1 to 1½-quart (950-ml to 1.4-liter) pan. Cook over medium-low heat, stirring, until jelly is melted. Baste turkey with some of the mixture, reserving remaining mixture.

4. Roast turkey in a 375°F (190°C) oven, basting with pan drippings and remaining jelly mixture, until a meat thermometer inserted in thickest part registers 160°F/70°C (about 2 hours); if drippings start to scorch, add ⅓ cup (80 ml) water to pan, stirring to loosen browned bits. Meanwhile, combine apple juice and 1⅓ cups (320 ml) of the broth in a 4- to 5-quart (3.8- to 5-liter) pan. Bring to a boil over high heat. Stir in pasta, cranberries, and coriander. Reduce heat, cover, and simmer, stirring occasionally, until almost all liquid is absorbed (about 15 minutes); do not scorch. Remove from heat and keep warm, stirring occasionally.

5. Transfer turkey to a warm platter; cover and let stand for 10 minutes. Meanwhile, pour pan drippings and accumulated juices into a 2 cup (470-ml) glass measure; skim off and discard fat. Stir cornstarch mixture and blend into drippings. Add enough of the remaining broth to make 1½ cups (360 ml). Pour into a 1- to 1½-quart (950-ml to 1.4-liter) pan and cook over medium-high heat, stirring, until boiling. Pour into a serving container.

6. Remove strings from turkey. Slice meat and arrange on individual plates. Stir parsley into pasta and mound beside turkey; sprinkle with nuts. Garnish with sage sprigs. Offer gravy, salt, and pepper to add to taste. Makes 8 to 10 servings.

Per serving: 456 calories (24% fat, 40% carbohydrates, 36% protein), 12 g total fat (3 g saturated), 45 g carbohydrates, 41 g protein, 93 mg cholesterol, 104 mg sodium

CHICKEN & SHRIMP PANSIT

Preparation time: About 25 minutes

Cooking time: About 45 minutes

Spiked with ginger, this specialty from the Philippines combines pasta, vegetables, chicken, and shrimp.

- 6 ounces (170 g) dried spaghetti
- 1 large onion (about 8 oz./230 g), finely chopped
- 4 cups (280 g) finely shredded cabbage
- 2 cups (280 g) diced cooked skinless chicken
- 1 cup (130 g) thinly sliced carrots
- ½ cup (120 ml) low-sodium chicken broth
- 1 tablespoon minced fresh ginger
- 4 cloves garlic, minced or pressed
- ¼ teaspoon pepper
- 3 tablespoons oyster sauce or 2 tablespoons reduced-sodium soy sauce (or to taste)
- 2 tablespoons seasoned rice vinegar (or 2 tablespoons distilled white vinegar and 1 teaspoon sugar) or to taste
- 4 green onions
- 8 ounces (230 g) tiny cooked shrimp
- 2 large hard-cooked eggs, shelled, cut into wedges (optional)

1. Bring 8 cups (1.9 liters) water to a boil in a 4- to 5-quart (3.8- to 5-liter) pan over medium-high heat. Stir in pasta and cook just until tender to bite (8 to 10 minutes); or cook according to package directions. Drain well and set aside.

2. Combine chopped onion and 2 tablespoons water in a wide nonstick frying pan over high heat. Cook, stirring often, until liquid has evaporated and browned bits stick to pan bottom. To deglaze pan, add ¼ cup (60 ml) more water, stirring to loosen browned bits. Continue to cook, stirring often, until liquid has evaporated and onion sticks to pan bottom again. Repeat deglazing step, adding ¼ cup (60 ml) more water each time, until onion is richly browned (about 15 minutes total).

3. Add pasta, cabbage, chicken, carrots, broth, ginger, garlic, and pepper to onion. Pour in oyster sauce and vinegar. Cook, stirring often, until liquid has evaporated and browned bits stick to pan bottom (about 10 minutes). Meanwhile, thinly slice 2 of the green onions; set aside.

4. Add ¼ cup (60 ml) water and remove from heat; stir to loosen browned bits. Transfer to a platter. Top with shrimp and sliced green onions. Garnish with remaining whole onions and, if desired, eggs. Makes 6 servings.

Per serving: 289 calories (14% fat, 47% carbohydrates, 39% protein), 5 g total fat (1 g saturated), 33 g carbohydrates, 28 g protein, 115 mg cholesterol, 605 mg sodium

VERMICELLI WITH TURKEY

Preparation time: About 15 minutes

Cooking time: About 15 minutes

This quick and colorful stir-fry is a whole meal in itself.

- 8 ounces (230 g) dried vermicelli
- ⅓ cup (40 g) dried tomatoes packed in oil, drained (reserve oil) and slivered
- 2 cloves garlic, minced or pressed
- 1 medium-size onion (about 6 oz./170 g), chopped
- 1 large yellow or red bell pepper (about 8 oz./230 g), chopped
- 3 medium-size zucchini (about 12 oz./340 g *total*), thinly sliced
- 1 cup (240 ml) low-sodium chicken broth
- 2 cups (280 g) shredded cooked turkey breast
- ½ cup (20 g) chopped fresh basil or 3 tablespoons dried basil
- Freshly grated Parmesan cheese

1. Bring 8 cups (1.9 liters) water to a boil in a 4- to 5-quart (3.8- to 5-liter) pan over medium-high heat. Stir in pasta and cook just until tender to bite (8 to 10 minutes); or cook according to package directions. Meanwhile, heat 1 tablespoon of the reserved oil from tomatoes in a wide nonstick frying pan over medium-high heat. Add tomatoes, garlic, onion, bell pepper, and zucchini. Cook, stirring often, until vegetables begin to brown (about 8 minutes).

2. Pour broth over vegetables and bring to a boil. Drain pasta well and add to vegetables with turkey and basil. Lift with 2 forks to mix. Transfer to a platter. Offer cheese to add to taste. Makes 4 servings.

Per serving: 502 calories (27% fat, 47% carbohydrates, 26% protein), 16 g total fat (2 g saturated), 59 g carbohydrates, 33 g protein, 59 mg cholesterol, 69 mg sodium

Roast Turkey with Apple Orzo ▶
(recipe on page 45)

Spaghetti with Turkey Meatballs

Preparation time: About 25 minutes

Cooking time: About 50 minutes

Trim the calories and fat of classic spaghetti and meatballs by making the meatballs from lean ground turkey.

- ¾ **cup (130 g) bulgur**
- 12 **ounces (340 g) ground turkey**
- 1 **large onion (about 8 oz./230 g), chopped**
- 4 **cloves garlic, minced or pressed**
- 1 **teaspoon dried oregano**
- ½ **teaspoon salt**
- ¼ **teaspoon pepper**
- 8 **ounces (230 g) mushrooms, sliced**
- 1 **tablespoon dried basil**
- ¼ **teaspoon crushed red pepper flakes**
  - **About 1¼ cups (300 ml) low-sodium chicken broth**
- 1 **can (about 28 oz./795 g) crushed tomatoes**
- 1 **pound (455 g) dried spaghetti**
  - **Chopped parsley**
  - **Freshly grated Parmesan cheese**

1. Mix bulgur with 1½ cups (360 ml) boiling water in a large bowl. Let stand just until bulgur is tender to bite (about 15 minutes). Drain well.

2. Combine turkey, onion, 2 cloves of the garlic, oregano, salt, pepper, and bulgur in a large bowl. Mix until blended. Shape into balls about ¼-cup (60-ml) size. Place slightly apart in a lightly oiled 10- by 15-inch (25- by 38-cm) baking pan. Bake in a 425°F (220°C) oven until well browned (25 to 30 minutes). Meanwhile, combine mushrooms, remaining 2 cloves garlic, basil, red pepper flakes, and ¼ cup (60 ml) water in a 5- to 6-quart (5- to 6-liter) pan. Cook over high heat, stirring often, until liquid has evaporated and mushrooms begin to brown (about 10 minutes). To deglaze pan, add ¼ cup (60 ml) of the broth, stirring to loosen browned bits. Continue to cook, stirring often, until liquid has evaporated and mushrooms begin to brown again. Repeat deglazing step, adding ¼ cup (60 ml) more broth each time, until mushrooms are well browned. Add tomatoes; reduce heat, cover, and simmer for 10 minutes.

3. Add meatballs to sauce mixture. Cover and simmer for 5 more minutes; add more broth if sauce sticks to pan bottom. Remove from heat and keep warm.

4. Bring 16 cups (3.8 liters) water to a boil in a 6- to 8-quart (6- to 8-liter) pan over medium-high heat. Stir in pasta and cook just until tender to bite (8 to 10 minutes); or cook according to package directions. Drain well.

5. Bring ⅓ cup (80 ml) more broth to a boil in pan. Add pasta and lift with 2 forks to mix. Pour into a wide serving bowl. Top with sauce and sprinkle with parsley. Offer cheese to add to taste. Makes 5 or 6 servings.

Per serving: 484 calories (12% fat, 67% carbohydrates, 21% protein), 7 g total fat (2 g saturated), 82 g carbohydrates, 25 g protein, 41 mg cholesterol, 474 mg sodium

Jamaican Jerk Chicken with Spiced Fettuccine

Preparation time: About 15 minutes

Marinating time: At least 30 minutes

Cooking time: About 20 minutes

Black peppercorns, hot red peppers, and fragrant spices all ground to a paste give jerk seasoning its intriguing complexity—and its bite.

- **Jerk Seasoning Paste (recipe follows)**
- 4 **skinless, boneless chicken breast halves (about 1½ lbs./680 g *total*)**
- 2 **cups (470 ml) low-sodium chicken broth**
- ¼ **cup (60 ml) whipping cream**
- 12 **ounces (340 g) dried fettuccine**
  - **Cilantro sprigs**
  - **Lime wedges**
  - **Salt**

1. Prepare Jerk Seasoning Paste. Cover and refrigerate 1 tablespoon of the paste. Coat chicken with remaining paste. Cover and refrigerate for at least 30 minutes or up to a day.

2. Combine broth, cream, and reserved 1 tablespoon paste in a wide nonstick frying pan. Bring to a boil over medium-high heat and cook until reduced to about 1½ cups/360 ml (about 10 minutes). Set aside.

3. Place chicken on a lightly oiled grill 4 to 6 inches (10 to 15 cm) above a solid bed of medium-hot coals. Grill, turning as needed, until chicken is no longer pink in center of thickest part; cut to test (8 to 10 minutes). Meanwhile, bring 12 cups (2.8 liters) water to a boil in a 5- to 6-quart (5- to 6-liter) pan over medium-high heat. Stir in pasta and cook just until tender to bite (8 to 10 minutes); or cook according to package directions. Drain pasta well, return to pan, and keep warm.

4. Transfer chicken to a platter and keep warm. Add broth mixture and any juices drained from chicken to pasta. Cook over medium heat, lifting with 2 forks, until most of the liquid is absorbed. Mound beside chicken. Garnish with cilantro. Offer lime and salt to add to taste. Makes 4 servings.

JERK SEASONING PASTE. In a blender or food processor, combine ¼ cup (10 g) firmly packed **cilantro**, 3 tablespoons *each* minced **fresh ginger** and **water**, 2 tablespoons **black peppercorns**, 1 tablespoon *each* **ground allspice** and firmly packed **brown sugar**, 2 cloves **garlic**, ½ teaspoon **crushed red pepper flakes**, and ¼ teaspoon *each* **ground coriander** and **ground nutmeg**. Whirl until smooth. If made ahead, cover and refrigerate for up to 2 days.

Per serving: 602 calories (17% fat, 47% carbohydrates, 36% protein), 11 g total fat (5 g saturated), 70 g carbohydrates, 53 g protein, 196 mg cholesterol, 165 mg sodium

FIVE-SPICE CHICKEN WITH PERCIATELLI

Preparation time: About 35 minutes

Cooking time: About 1 hour

Fragrant Chinese five-spice stars in this entrée.

- 2 ounces (55 g) dried shiitake mushrooms
- 1 clove garlic, minced or pressed
- 1½ teaspoons Chinese five-spice; or ½ teaspoon *each* anise seeds and ground ginger and ¼ teaspoon *each* ground cinnamon and ground cloves
- 3 tablespoons reduced-sodium soy sauce
- 1 tablespoon *each* sugar and dry sherry
- 1 chicken (4½ to 5 lbs./2 to 2.3 kg)

- 14 ounces (400 g) dried perciatelli, bucatini, or spaghetti
- 1¼ pounds (565 g) broccoli flowerets
  Oriental Dressing (recipe follows)
- 3 tablespoons minced green onions
  Salt and pepper

1. Soak mushrooms in boiling water to cover until soft (about 20 minutes). Lift out and squeeze dry; discard liquid. Cut off and discard coarse stems. Slice in half, if desired. Place in a large bowl and set aside.

2. Combine garlic, five-spice, and 1 tablespoon water in a small nonstick frying pan over medium heat. Cook, stirring, just until fragrant and hot; do not scorch. Remove from heat and add soy sauce, sugar and sherry; stir until blended.

3. Rinse chicken and pat dry; reserve giblets for other uses. Place chicken, breast side up, on a rack in a 9- by 13-inch (23- by 33-cm) baking pan. Baste with five-spice mixture. Pour remaining mixture into cavity. Roast in a 375°F (190°C) oven until meat near thighbone is no longer pink; cut to test (about 1 hour); if drippings begin to scorch, add ⅓ cup (80 ml) water, stirring to loosen browned bits. Meanwhile bring 16 cups (3.8 liters) water to a boil in a 6- to 8-quart (6- to 8-liter) pan over medium-high heat. Stir in pasta and cook for 7 minutes. Add broccoli and cook, stirring occasionally, just until pasta is tender to bite and broccoli is tender-crisp (about 5 more minutes). Drain well and transfer to bowl with mushrooms; keep warm.

4. Prepare Oriental Dressing. Pour warm dressing over pasta; gently lift with 2 forks to mix. Keep warm.

5. Lift out chicken, draining juices into pan, and place on a platter. Stir juices to loosen browned bits. Pour into a serving container and skim off and discard fat; add onions. Mound pasta around chicken. Offer juices, salt, and pepper to add to taste. Makes 6 to 8 servings.

ORIENTAL DRESSING. In a 1- to 1½-quart (950-ml to 1.4-liter) pan, combine ½ cup (120 ml) **seasoned rice vinegar** (or ½ cup/120 ml rice vinegar and 4 teaspoons sugar); 3 tablespoons **reduced-sodium soy sauce;** 1 teaspoon **ground coriander;** and 1 or 2 cloves **garlic,** minced or pressed. Season to taste with **crushed red pepper flakes.** Bring just to a boil over medium heat. Use warm. Makes about ⅔ cup (160 ml).

Per serving: 615 calories (29% fat, 39% carbohydrates, 32% protein), 20 g total fat (5 g saturated), 60 g carbohydrates, 49 g protein, 119 mg cholesterol, 989 mg sodium

TURKEY SAUSAGE WITH PENNE

Pictured on facing page

Preparation time: About 15 minutes

Cooking time: About 20 minutes

For a nutritious dinner you can prepare in minutes, toss together vegetables and pasta with a tangy fennel-accented sausage sauce.

- 12   ounces (340 g) spinach, coarse stems removed, rinsed and drained
- 1   large red or yellow bell pepper (about 8 oz./ 230 g), seeded
- 3   green onions
- 8   ounces/230 g (about 2½ cups) dried penne
- 8   to 12 ounces (230 to 340 g) mild or hot turkey Italian sausages, casings removed
- ½   cup (120 ml) balsamic vinegar; or ½ cup (120 ml) red wine vinegar and 5 teaspoons sugar
- ½   to ¾ teaspoon fennel seeds
   Salt and pepper

1. Tear spinach into pieces. Cut bell pepper lengthwise into thin strips. Cut onions into 3-inch (8-cm) lengths and sliver lengthwise. Place vegetables in a large serving bowl and set aside.

2. Bring 8 cups (1.9 liters) water to a boil in a 4- to 5-quart (3.8- to 5-liter) pan over medium-high heat. Stir in pasta and cook just until tender to bite (8 to 10 minutes); or cook according to package directions. Drain well and keep warm.

3. Chop or crumble sausages. Cook in a wide nonstick frying pan over medium-high heat, stirring often, until browned (about 10 minutes). Add vinegar and fennel seeds, stirring to loosen browned bits.

4. Add pasta to vegetables and immediately pour on sausage mixture; toss until spinach is slightly wilted. Serve immediately. Offer salt and pepper to add to taste. Makes 6 servings.

Per serving: 238 calories (22% fat, 54% carbohydrates, 24% protein), 6 g total fat (2 g saturated), 32 g carbohydrates, 15 g protein, 36 mg cholesterol, 327 mg sodium

ONE-PAN TURKEY SAUSAGE & ORZO CASSEROLE

Preparation time: About 15 minutes

Cooking time: About 1 hour and 10 minutes

Orzo cooked with broth in the oven gains flavor from tomatoes and sausages.

- 1   can (about 28 oz./795 g) tomatoes
   About ¾ cup (180 ml) beef broth
- 8   ounces (230 g) *each* mild and hot turkey Italian sausages, casings removed, sliced ¼ inch (6 mm) thick
- 2   large onions (about 1 lb./455 g *total*), minced
- 2   tablespoons chopped fresh basil or 2 teaspoons dried basil
- 12   ounces/340 g (about 2 cups) dried orzo or other rice-shaped pasta
- ¼   cup (30 g) shredded part-skim mozzarella cheese

1. Break up tomatoes with a spoon and drain juice into a 1-quart (950-ml) measure; reserve tomatoes. Add enough broth to juice to make 3 cups (710 ml); set aside.

2. Place sausages and onions in a shallow 2½- to 3-quart (2.4- to 2.8-liter) casserole. Bake in a 450°F (230°C) oven, stirring occasionally to loosen browned bits, until well browned (about 45 minutes). Remove from oven. Add tomatoes, broth mixture, and basil, stirring to loosen browned bits. Return to oven and continue to bake until mixture comes to a boil (about 10 minutes).

3. Remove from oven and stir in pasta. Cover tightly with foil, return to oven, and continue to bake until liquid is absorbed and pasta is tender to bite (about 15 minutes). Sprinkle with cheese. Makes 6 servings.

Per serving: 407 calories (22% fat, 54% carbohydrates, 24% protein), 10 g total fat (3 g saturated), 55 g carbohydrates, 24 g protein, 60 mg cholesterol, 812 mg sodium

◄ *Turkey Sausage with Penne (recipe above)*

Nowhere is the versatility of pasta more evident than when you consider the variety of sauces that can accompany it. Here's a selection of four light sauces. All can be made ahead and refrigerated or frozen; simply reheat (thaw first, if necessary) and serve with hot pasta for a delicious meal that takes only minutes to make.

Pair the robust vegetable and meat sauces with the heavier pastas, such as spaghetti, fettuccine, and rigatoni. Delicate sauces, such as the Roasted Red Pepper Sauce, go well with vermicelli, capellini, shells, or the homemade pastas on pages 20–21. Or experiment with your own combinations. At the table, offer Parmesan cheese, if desired.

Although some of these sauces get more than 30 percent of their calories from fat, they still have a place in a nutritious, low-fat diet when paired with pasta and other low-fat ingredients.

SWEET SPICE MEAT SAUCE

Preparation time: About 20 minutes

Cooking time: About 1⅔ hours

Spice Blend (recipe follows)

4 **slices bacon, chopped**

1 **pound (455 g) lean ground beef**

4 **medium-size onions (about 1½ lbs./680 g *total*), chopped**

1 **cup (120 g) finely chopped celery**

2 **cloves garlic, minced or pressed**

2 **tablespoons minced parsley**

3 **cans (about 15 oz./425 g *each*) tomato sauce**

1 **can (about 6 oz./170 g) tomato paste**

2 **tablespoons red wine vinegar**

1. Prepare Spice Blend.

2. Combine bacon and beef in a 5- to 6-quart (5- to 6-liter) pan. Cook over medium-high heat, stirring often, until well browned (about 15 minutes).

3. Pour off fat. Add onions, celery, garlic, parsley, and Spice Blend. Cook, stirring often, until onions are soft (about 20 minutes).

4. Add tomato sauce, tomato paste, and vinegar; stir well. Bring to a boil; reduce heat and simmer until reduced to about 8 cups/1.9 liters (about 1 hour). If made ahead, let cool and then cover and refrigerate for up to 2 days; reheat before using. Makes about 8 cups (1.9 liters).

SPICE BLEND. In small bowl, combine 1 tablespoon firmly packed **brown sugar;** ½ teaspoon *each* **ground cinnamon, dried oregano, pepper, rubbed sage,** and **dried thyme;** and ¼ teaspoon *each* **ground cloves** and **ground nutmeg.** Mix until blended.

ROASTED RED PEPPER SAUCE

Preparation time: About 10 minutes

Cooking time: About 20 minutes

Roasted Red Bell Peppers (directions follow)

1 **teaspoon olive oil**

1 **large onion (about 8 oz./230 g), chopped**

3 **cloves garlic, minced or pressed**

2 **tablespoons dry sherry (or to taste)**

1 **tablespoon white wine vinegar (or to taste)**

⅛ **teaspoon ground white pepper**

¼ **cup (20 g) freshly grated Parmesan cheese**
   Salt

1. Prepare Roasted Red Bell Peppers. Set aside with any drippings in a blender or food processor.

2. Heat oil in a wide nonstick frying pan over medium-high heat. Add onion and garlic. Cook, stirring often, until onion is soft (about 5 minutes); if pan appears dry or onion mixture sticks to pan bottom, add water, 1 tablespoon at a time.

3. Transfer onion mixture to blender with peppers. Whirl until smooth. Add sherry, vinegar, and pepper. Whirl until of desired consistency. (At this point, you may cover and refrigerate for up to 2 days; reheat before continuing.)

4. Add cheese. Season to taste with salt. Makes about 3 cups (710 ml).

ROASTED RED BELL PEPPERS. Cut 4 large **red bell peppers** (about 2 lbs./905 g *total*) in half lengthwise. Place, cut sides down, in a 10- by 15-inch (25- by 38-cm) baking pan. Broil 4 to 6 inches (10 to 15 cm) below heat, turning as needed, until charred all over (about 8 minutes). Cover with foil and let cool in pan. Pull off and discard skins, stems, and seeds. Cut into chunks.

TURKEY ITALIAN SAUSAGE SAUCE

Preparation time: About 10 minutes

Cooking time: About 40 minutes

1   **pound (455 g) mild or hot turkey Italian sausages, casings removed, or Low-fat Italian Sausage (page 19)**

1   **large onion (about 8 oz./ 230 g), chopped**

3   **cloves garlic, minced or pressed**

1   **can (about 29 oz./820 g) tomato purée**

3   **tablespoons chopped fresh basil or 1 tablespoon dried basil**

½   **teaspoon fennel seeds**

2   **tablespoons dry red wine (or to taste)**

   Salt and pepper

1. Chop or crumble sausages. Place in a 4- to 5-quart (3.8- to 5-liter) pan with onion, garlic, and 2 tablespoons water. Cook over medium heat, stirring often, until sausage mixture is well browned (about 15 minutes); if pan appears dry or sausage mixture sticks to pan bottom, add water, 1 tablespoon at a time.

2. Stir in tomato purée, basil, and fennel seeds. Increase heat to medium-high and bring to a boil; reduce heat and simmer until reduced to about 4½ cups/1 liter (about 20 minutes).

3. Remove from heat and add wine. Season to taste with salt and pepper. If made ahead, let cool and then cover and refrigerate for up to 2 days; reheat before using. Makes about 4½ cups (1 liter).

PORCINI-TOMATO SAUCE

Preparation time: About 35 minutes

Cooking time: About 1½ hours

⅔   **ounce (20 g) dried porcini mushrooms (about ⅔ cup)**

8   **ounces (230 g) pancetta or bacon, finely chopped**

1   **large onion (about 8 oz./ 230 g), finely chopped**

2   **small carrots (about 4 oz./ 115 g *total*), finely chopped**

2   **large stalks celery (about 8 oz./230 g *total*), finely chopped**

2   **cloves garlic, minced or pressed**

¼   **cup (15 g) finely chopped parsley**

1   **can (about 15 oz./425 g) chopped or puréed tomatoes**

2   **cups (470 ml) beef broth**

1   **can (about 6 oz./170 g) tomato paste**

   Salt

1. Soak mushrooms in 1½ cups (360 ml) boiling water until soft (about 20 minutes). Lift out and squeeze dry. Chop finely and set aside. Without disturbing sediment at bottom, pour soaking liquid into a measuring cup and set aside. Discard sediment.

2. Cook pancetta in a 5- to 6-quart (5- to 6-liter) pan over medium-high heat, stirring often, until browned and crisp (7 to 10 minutes). Add onion, carrots, celery, garlic, and parsley. Cook, stirring often, until vegetables begin to brown and stick to pan bottom (7 to 10 more minutes).

3. Stir in tomatoes and their liquid, broth, tomato paste, mushrooms, and reserved soaking liquid. Bring to a boil; reduce heat and simmer until reduced to about 6 cups/ 1.4 liters (about 1 hour).

4. Season to taste with salt. If made ahead, let cool and then cover and refrigerate for up to 2 days; reheat before using. Makes about 6 cups (1.4 liters).

LINGCOD WITH CITRUS ALMOND COUSCOUS

Pictured on facing page

Preparation time: About 30 minutes

Cooking time: About 20 minutes

A medley of citrus fruits accents this pasta dish.

- 5 or 6 small oranges (about 2½ lbs./1.15 kg *total*)
- 1 large pink grapefruit (about 12 oz./340 g)
- 1 medium-size lemon (about 5 oz./140 g)
- 1 medium-size lime (about 3 oz./85 g)
- ¼ cup (30 g) slivered almonds
- 2 tablespoons olive oil
- ¼ cup (45 g) chopped onion
- ½ teaspoon almond extract
- 10 ounces/285 g (about 1⅔ cups) dried couscous
- 2 pounds (905 g) skinless, boneless lingcod or striped bass fillets (*each* about 1 inch/2.5 cm thick)
- ¼ cup (60 ml) rice vinegar
- 2 tablespoons minced shallots

1. Shred enough peel from oranges and grapefruit to make 1½ tablespoons each. Shred enough peel from lemon and lime to make 1 teaspoon each. Combine peels in a small bowl; set aside. Remove remaining peel and white membrane from grapefruit, lemon, lime, and 2 of the oranges. Over a bowl, cut between membranes to release segments. In a separate bowl, juice remaining oranges to make 1½ cups (360 ml). Set bowls aside.

2. Toast almonds in a 2- to 3-quart (1.9- to 2.8-liter) pan over medium heat, shaking pan often, until golden (about 4 minutes). Remove from pan and set aside. Place 2 teaspoons of the oil in pan and heat over medium-high heat. Add onion and cook, stirring often, until soft (about 3 minutes). Add 1 cup (240 ml) of the orange juice, 1½ cups (360 ml) water, and almond extract. Bring to a boil. Stir in pasta; cover, remove from heat, and let stand until liquid is absorbed (about 5 minutes). Keep warm, fluffing occasionally with a fork.

3. Cut fish into 6 portions and brush with 2 teaspoons more oil. Place on rack of a 12- by 14-inch (30- by 35.5-cm) broiler pan. Broil about 4 inches (10 cm) below heat, turning once, just until opaque but still moist in thickest part; cut to test (about 10 minutes).

4. Combine remaining ½ cup (120 ml) orange juice and 2 teaspoons oil, vinegar, shallots, fruit, and accumulated juices in a wide nonstick frying pan. Cook over medium heat, stirring often, until warm (about 2 minutes).

5. Arrange pasta and fish on individual plates. Top fish with fruit sauce and sprinkle almonds over pasta. Garnish with citrus peel. Makes 6 servings.

Per serving: 457 calories (19% fat, 50% carbohydrates, 31% protein), 10 g total fat (1 g saturated), 58 g carbohydrates, 35 g protein, 79 mg cholesterol, 98 mg sodium

COUSCOUS PAELLA

Preparation time: About 15 minutes

Cooking time: 20 to 25 minutes

Although traditionally based on rice, this paella is made with quick-cooking couscous.

- 4 ounces (115 g) chorizo sausages, casings removed
- 1 large onion (about 8 oz./230 g), chopped
- 1 bottle (about 8 oz./240 ml) clam juice
- 1¼ cups (300 ml) low-sodium chicken broth
- 2 teaspoons cumin seeds
- 9¼ ounces /260 g (about 1½ cups) dried couscous
- 1 medium-size red bell pepper (about 6 oz./170 g), seeded and chopped
- 8 ounces (230 g) tiny cooked shrimp
  Lime or lemon wedges

1. Crumble chorizo into a wide nonstick frying pan; add onion. Cook over medium heat, stirring often, until well browned (15 to 20 minutes); if pan appears dry or mixture sticks to pan bottom, add water, 1 tablespoon at a time.

2. Add clam juice, broth, and cumin seeds. Increase heat to medium-high and bring to a boil. Stir in pasta; cover, remove from heat, and let stand until liquid is absorbed (about 5 minutes). Transfer to a wide serving bowl.

3. Stir in bell pepper and top with shrimp. Offer lime to add to taste. Makes 4 to 6 servings.

Per serving: 378 calories (24% fat, 51% carbohydrates, 25% protein), 10 g total fat (4 g saturated), 47 g carbohydrates, 23 g protein, 106 mg cholesterol, 227 mg sodium

Lingcod with Citrus Almond Couscous ▶ (recipe above left)

HALIBUT PICCATA WITH LEMON LINGUINE

Preparation time: About 15 minutes

Cooking time: About 25 minutes

Succulent halibut fillets are quickly broiled and then served with lemony linguine.

- 1 teaspoon olive oil
- 2 cloves garlic, minced or pressed
- ⅔ cup (160 ml) dry white wine
- ⅓ cup (80 ml) lemon juice
- 2 tablespoons drained capers
- 8 ounces (230 g) dried linguine
- 1½ pounds (680 g) Pacific halibut fillets (*each* ¾ to 1 inch/2 to 2.5 cm thick)

  Pepper
- ¼ cup (20 g) freshly grated Parmesan cheese
- ½ cup (120 ml) low-sodium chicken broth
- ½ teaspoon grated lemon peel
- 2 teaspoons honey
- 1 teaspoon Dijon mustard
- 2 ounces/55 g Neufchâtel or cream cheese
- ¼ cup (15 g) minced parsley

1. Heat oil in a small nonstick frying pan over medium-high heat. Add garlic and cook, stirring, until fragrant and hot; do not scorch. Add ½ cup (120 ml) of the wine, 3 tablespoons of the lemon juice, and capers. Bring to a boil and cook until reduced to about ½ cup/120 ml (about 4 minutes). Remove from heat and keep warm.

2. Bring 8 cups (1.9 liters) water to a boil in a 4- to 5-quart (3.8- to 5-liter) pan over medium-high heat. Stir in pasta and cook just until tender to bite (8 to 10 minutes); or cook according to package directions. Drain well and keep warm.

3. Cut fish into 4 equal portions and sprinkle with pepper. Place in a single layer in a lightly oiled broiler pan without a rack. Broil about 3 inches (8 cm) below heat for 3 minutes. Turn, sprinkle with Parmesan cheese, and continue to broil until opaque but still moist in center of thickest part; cut to test (about 3 more minutes). Keep warm.

4. Combine broth, lemon peel, remaining lemon juice, honey, and mustard in a 3- to 4-quart (2.8- to 3.8-liter) pan. Bring to a boil over high heat. Remove from heat; whisk in Neufchâtel cheese just until melted. Add pasta, remaining wine, and parsley; lift with 2 forks to mix. Mound on individual plates. Arrange fish alongside; drizzle with sauce. Makes 4 servings.

Per serving: 523 calories (21% fat, 40% carbohydrates, 39% protein), 11 g total fat (4 g saturated), 49 g carbohydrates, 47 g protein, 70 mg cholesterol, 428 mg sodium

FETTUCCINE WITH SHRIMP & GORGONZOLA

Preparation time: About 10 minutes

Cooking time: About 15 minutes

Just a little Gorgonzola packs a big punch in this entrée.

- 12 ounces (340 g) dried spinach or regular fettuccine
- 2 teaspoons butter or margarine
- 12 ounces (340 g) mushrooms, sliced
- ¾ cup (180 ml) half-and-half
- 3 ounces/85 g (about ⅔ cup) Gorgonzola cheese, crumbled
- ¾ cup (180 ml) low-sodium chicken broth
- 8 ounces (230 g) tiny cooked shrimp
- 2 tablespoons minced parsley

1. Bring 12 cups (2.8 liters) water to a boil in a 5- to 6-quart (5- to 6-liter) pan over medium-high heat. Stir in pasta and cook just until tender to bite (8 to 10 minutes); or cook according to package directions. Drain well and keep warm.

2. Melt butter in a wide nonstick frying pan over medium-high heat. Add mushrooms and cook, stirring often, until browned (about 8 minutes). Add half-and-half, cheese, and broth. Reduce heat to medium and cook, stirring, until cheese is melted (about 2 minutes); do not boil.

3. Add shrimp and pasta quickly. Lift with 2 forks until most of the liquid is absorbed. Transfer to a platter. Sprinkle with parsley. Makes 6 servings.

Per serving: 373 calories (29% fat, 48% carbohydrates, 23% protein), 12 g total fat (6 g saturated), 44 g carbohydrates, 22 g protein, 153 mg cholesterol, 358 mg sodium

SALMON WITH ASIAN-STYLE CAPELLINI

Pictured on page 95

Preparation time: About 40 minutes

Cooking time: About 10 minutes

Chilling time: At least 30 minutes

The combination of rice vinegar, soy sauce, and Oriental sesame oil is popular in Asian cooking. In this easy-to-fix entrée, the sweet-tart flavors enhance tender pasta and crisp greens. Hot grilled salmon fillets complete the presentation.

- 8 **ounces (230 g) dried capellini**
- 5 **tablespoons (75 ml) seasoned rice vinegar; or 5 tablespoons (75 ml) distilled white vinegar and 2 tablespoons sugar**
- 5 **tablespoons (75 ml) lime juice**
- 5 **teaspoons Oriental sesame oil**
- ¼ **teaspoon ground red pepper (cayenne)**
- 2 **teaspoons reduced-sodium soy sauce**
- ½ **cup (50 g) thinly sliced green onions**
- 5½ **to 6 ounces (155 to 170 g) mixed salad greens, rinsed and crisped**
- 1 **cup (40 g) *each* firmly packed cilantro and fresh basil, chopped**
- 1 **large cucumber (about 12 oz./340 g), peeled, cut in half lengthwise, seeded, and thinly sliced crosswise**
- 4 **thin boneless, skinless baby salmon fillets (about 6 oz./170 g *each*)**

    Lime slices

    Basil sprigs

1. Bring 8 cups (1.9 liters) water to a boil in a 4- to 5-quart (3.8- to 5-liter) pan over medium-high heat. Stir in pasta and cook just until tender to bite (about 4 minutes); or cook according to package directions. Drain, rinse with cold water, and drain well.

2. Mix 3 tablespoons each of the vinegar and lime juice, 4 teaspoons of the oil, ground red pepper, soy sauce, and onions in a large bowl. Add pasta, lifting with 2 forks to mix. Cover and refrigerate until cool (at least 30 minutes); mix occasionally.

3. Mix greens, cilantro, chopped basil, and remaining 2 tablespoons vinegar in a large bowl. Arrange on individual plates. Top with pasta and cucumber. Set aside.

4. Stir remaining 2 tablespoons lime juice with remaining 1 teaspoon oil. Brush mixture over both sides of each fish fillet.

5. Place fillets on rack of a 12- by 15-inch (30- by 38-cm) broiler pan. Broil about 4 inches (10 cm) below heat, turning once, just until opaque but still moist in thickest part; cut to test (about 4 minutes).

6. Place a hot fish fillet over pasta on each plate. Garnish with lime slices and basil sprigs. Makes 4 servings.

Per serving: 566 calories (29% fat, 40% carbohydrates, 31% protein), 18 g total fat (3 g saturated), 57 g carbohydrates, 44 g protein, 94 mg cholesterol, 568 mg sodium

Linguine with Lemon-Basil Seafood

Pictured on facing page

Preparation time: About 1 hour

Cooking time: About 30 minutes

This spectacular entrée of assorted shellfish is presented on a bed of linguine. Steeping the shrimp, scallops, and mussels helps to preserve their delicate flavors and textures. To complete this very fine meal, you need add only a beverage and warm loaves of your favorite crusty bread.

- 3 **cups (710 ml) low-sodium chicken broth**
- 1½ **cups (360 ml) dry white wine**
- 2 **pounds (905 g) large shrimp (31 to 35 per lb.), shelled and deveined**
- 1 **pound (455 g) bay scallops, rinsed and drained**
- 36 **to 48 small mussels or small hard-shell clams in shell, suitable for steaming, scrubbed**
  Lemon-Basil Dressing (recipe follows)
- 2 **pounds (905 g) dried linguine**
- 3 **tablespoons chopped parsley**
  Thin lemon slices

1. Combine broth, wine, and 2 cups (470 ml) water in a 6- to 8-quart (6- to 8-liter) pan. Bring to a boil over high heat. Add shrimp. Cover tightly, remove from heat, and let stand just until shrimp are opaque in center; cut to test (about 3 minutes). With a slotted spoon, transfer shrimp to a large bowl; keep warm.

2. Return broth to a boil. Add scallops. Cover tightly, remove from heat, and let stand just until scallops are opaque in center; cut to test (about 3 minutes). With a slotted spoon, transfer scallops to bowl with shrimp; keep warm.

3. Return broth to a boil. Add mussels; reduce heat, cover, and boil gently until shells pop open (5 to 10 minutes). With a slotted spoon, transfer mussels to bowl with seafood; discard any unopened shells.

4. Pour broth from pan into a 2-quart (1.9-liter) measure, leaving sediment in pan. Measure 1¾ cups (420 ml) of the broth and reserve for dressing. Drain any liquid from cooked seafood into remaining broth; reserve for other uses.

5. Prepare Lemon-Basil Dressing. Add 1 cup (240 ml) of the dressing to seafood and stir gently. Keep warm.

6. Bring 20 cups (5 liters) water to a boil in an 8- to 10-quart (8- to 10-liter) pan over medium-high heat. Stir in pasta, half at a time, if desired, and cook just until tender to bite (8 to 10 minutes); or cook according to package directions. Drain well and transfer to a very large (15- by 21-inch/38- by 53-cm or round 16-inch/41-cm) platter or shallow bowl. Add remaining dressing and lift with 2 forks to mix.

7. Mound seafood over pasta, arranging mussel shells around edge of platter, if desired. Sprinkle with parsley and garnish with lemon. Makes 10 to 12 servings.

LEMON-BASIL DRESSING. In a 1- to 1½-quart (950-ml to 1.4-liter) pan, stir together 1 tablespoon finely shredded **lemon peel,** ¾ cup (180 ml) **lemon juice,** 1¾ cups (420 ml) **reserved broth** from seafood, ¼ cup (60 ml) **olive oil,** 3 tablespoons **honey,** and 1½ teaspoons coarsely ground **pepper.** Bring to a boil over medium heat. Remove from heat and stir in ½ cup (80 g) minced **shallots,** 2 tablespoons chopped **fresh basil** or 2 teaspoons dried basil, and 2 or 3 cloves **garlic,** minced or pressed. Keep warm.

Per serving: 518 calories (15% fat, 57% carbohydrates, 28% protein), 9 g total fat (1 g saturated), 71 g carbohydrates, 35 g protein, 124 mg cholesterol, 266 mg sodium

◄ *Linguine with Lemon-Basil Seafood*
(recipe above)

PASTA SIDE DISHES

Because it's so versatile, pasta can play a variety of roles in menu planning. Here are several recipes that are ideal accompaniments for unadorned main dishes, such as roast chicken, broiled fish steaks, and grilled meat.

Creamy Pasta Pilaf can be prepared with any small pasta shape, such as rice-shaped pasta (riso or orzo), tiny bows, or whimsical stars. The relish that tops the pancake in Crisp Pasta Pancake with Spicy Pepper Relish must cool slightly before serving; the spicy caramelized peppers get very hot and can burn your mouth. Ravioli with Mushrooms, Carrots & Zucchini is full of fresh vegetables; it's hearty enough to satisfy two as a main course. Offer Spanish-style Linguine with roasted meat or poultry.

Other recipes throughout this book can be adapted to serve as side dishes. Some can be offered just as they are, but in smaller portions. With some others, just eliminate the meat or fish.

PASTA PILAF

Preparation time: About 15 minutes

Cooking time: About 20 minutes

- 1 **tablespoon butter or margarine**
- 1 **large onion (about 8 oz./ 230 g), finely chopped**
- 1 **clove garlic, minced or pressed**
- 6 **medium-size pear-shaped (Roma-type) tomatoes (about 12 oz./340 g *total*), peeled, seeded, and chopped**
- 1 **tablespoon chopped fresh basil or 1 teaspoon dried basil**

- 8 **ounces/230 g (about 1 cup) dried riso, stars, or other small pasta shape**
- ¾ **cup (110 g) frozen peas**
- ½ **cup (120 ml) half-and-half**
- ½ **cup (40 g) freshly grated Parmesan cheese**

1. Melt butter in a wide nonstick frying pan over medium heat. Add onion and garlic. Cook, stirring occasionally, until onion is soft (about 5 minutes).

2. Add tomatoes, basil, and ¼ cup (60 ml) water; reduce heat, cover, and simmer for 10 minutes. Meanwhile, bring 8 cups (1.9 liters) water to a boil in a 4- to 5-quart (3.8- to 5-liter) pan over medium-high heat. Stir in pasta and cook just until tender to bite (8 to 10 minutes); or cook according to package directions. Drain well.

3. Add peas and half-and-half to pan with tomato mixture. Increase heat to high and bring to a boil; stir in pasta. Remove from heat and stir in ¼ cup (20 g) of the cheese. Transfer to a serving dish. Offer remaining ¼ cup (20 g) cheese to add to taste. Makes 4 to 6 servings.

Per serving: 305 calories (25% fat, 59% carbohydrates, 16% protein), 9 g total fat (5 g saturated), 45 g carbohydrates, 12 g protein, 21 mg cholesterol, 217 mg sodium

CRISP PASTA PANCAKE WITH SPICY PEPPER RELISH

Preparation time: About 20 minutes

Cooking time: About 30 minutes

- 2 *each* **large red and yellow bell peppers (about 2 lbs./905 g *total*)**
- 8 **fresh green or red serrano chiles (about 2 oz./55 g *total*)**
- 1 **cup (200 g) sugar**
- ⅔ **cup (160 ml) distilled white vinegar**
- 8 **ounces (230 g) fresh capellini**
- 1 **tablespoon Oriental sesame oil**
- 2 **teaspoons salad oil**

1. Seed bell peppers and chiles; cut into thin strips. Transfer to a large bowl and add sugar and vinegar. Mix well.

2. Spoon pepper mixture into a wide nonstick frying pan. Cook over medium heat, stirring often, until most of the liquid has evaporated (about 30 minutes). Meanwhile, bring 8 cups (1.9 liters) water to a boil in a 4- to 5-quart (3.8- to 5-liter) pan over medium-high heat.

Stir in pasta and cook just until tender to bite (about 45 seconds); or cook according to package directions. Drain well. Transfer to a bowl, sprinkle with sesame oil, and lift with 2 forks to mix. Place a 12-inch (30-cm) pizza pan in oven while it heats to 500°F (260°C). When pan is hot (about 5 minutes), pour in salad oil, tilting pan to coat. Spread pasta in pan and bake on lowest rack until golden (about 20 minutes).

3. Slide pancake onto a platter. Spread pepper mixture on top. Cut into wedges. Makes 8 servings.

Per serving: 257 calories (12% fat, 81% carbohydrates, 7% protein), 3 g total fat (0.5 g saturated), 54 g carbohydrates, 5 g protein, 0 mg cholesterol, 5 mg sodium

RAVIOLI WITH MUSHROOMS, CARROTS & ZUCCHINI

Preparation time: About 15 minutes

Cooking time: About 12 minutes

1 tablespoon butter or margarine

8 ounces (230 g) mushrooms, finely chopped

2 large carrots (about 8 oz./230 g *total*), finely shredded

2 medium-size zucchini (about 8 oz./230 g *total*), finely shredded

3 cloves garlic, minced or pressed

1 tablespoon minced fresh basil or 1 teaspoon dried basil

½ cup (105 g) low-fat (1%) cottage cheese

¾ cup (180 ml) nonfat milk

1 package (about 9 oz./255 g) fresh low-fat or regular cheese ravioli

1. Melt butter in a wide nonstick frying pan over medium-high heat. Add mushrooms, carrots, zucchini, garlic, and basil. Cook, stirring often, until liquid has evaporated (about 10 minutes).

2. Place cottage cheese and ¼ cup (60 ml) of the milk in a blender or food processor. Whirl until smooth. Spoon into pan with vegetables and stir in remaining ½ cup (120 ml) milk. Cook over medium heat, stirring often, just until sauce begins to boil (about 2 minutes). Remove from heat and keep warm.

3. Bring 12 cups (2.8 liters) water to a boil in a 5- to 6-quart (5- to 6-liter) pan over medium-high heat. Separating any ravioli that are stuck together, stir in pasta and cook just until tender to bite (4 to 6 minutes); or cook according to package directions. Drain well. Transfer to a large serving bowl. Add sauce and mix thoroughly but gently. Makes 6 servings.

Per serving: 190 calories (23% fat, 53% carbohydrates, 24% protein), 5 g total fat (2 g saturated), 26 g carbohydrates, 12 g protein, 34 mg cholesterol, 283 mg sodium

SPANISH-STYLE LINGUINE

Preparation time: About 10 minutes

Cooking time: About 15 minutes

8 ounces (230 g) dried linguine

1 jar (about 6 oz./170 g) marinated artichokes, quartered

2 cloves garlic, minced or pressed

1 tablespoon anchovy paste

1 can (about 2¼ oz./65 g) sliced black ripe olives, drained

½ cup (30 g) chopped parsley
  Pepper
  Freshly grated Parmesan cheese

1. Bring 8 cups (1.9 liters) water to a boil in a 4- to 5-quart (3.8- to 5-liter) pan over medium-high heat. Stir in pasta and cook just until tender to bite (8 to 10 minutes); or cook according to package directions. Meanwhile, drain marinade from artichokes into a 1½- to 2-quart (1.4- to 1.9-liter) pan. Place over medium heat. Add garlic and cook, stirring often, until pale golden (about 3 minutes). Add anchovy paste, olives, and artichokes. Cook, stirring gently, until hot (about 2 minutes).

2. Drain pasta well and return to pan. Add artichoke mixture and parsley. Lift with 2 forks to mix. Transfer pasta to a large serving bowl. Offer pepper and cheese to add to taste. Makes 4 to 6 servings.

Per serving: 227 calories (20% fat, 66% carbohydrates, 14% protein), 5 g total fat (0.7 g saturated), 38 g carbohydrates, 8 g protein, 2 mg cholesterol, 424 mg sodium

CRAB WITH EMERALD SAUCE

Pictured on facing page

Preparation time: About 20 minutes

Cooking time: About 8 minutes

A bright green sauce puréed from fresh basil and cilantro cradles delicate pasta and chunks of fresh crab.

- 8 ounces (230 g) basil sprigs; or 6 ounces (170 g) spinach and ¼ cup (8 g) dried basil
- 4 ounces (115 g) cilantro sprigs
- 8 ounces (230 g) dried capellini
- ¼ cup (60 ml) seasoned rice vinegar; or ¼ cup (60 ml) rice vinegar and 1 teaspoon sugar
- 1 tablespoon *each* minced lemon peel and Oriental sesame oil
- ¾ cup (180 ml) low-sodium chicken broth
- 2 tablespoons salad oil
- ⅓ to ½ pound (150 to 230 g) cooked crabmeat

1. Reserve 4 of the basil or cilantro sprigs for garnish.

2. Bring 8 cups (1.9 liters) water to a boil in a 4- to 5-quart (3.8- to 5-liter) pan over medium-high heat. Gather half the remaining fresh basil (or spinach) into a bunch. Holding stem ends with tongs, dip leaves into boiling water just until bright green (about 3 seconds). At once plunge into ice water. Repeat with cilantro and remaining basil.

3. Stir pasta into water and cook just until tender to bite (about 4 minutes); or cook according to package directions. Drain well. Place in a bowl. Add vinegar, lemon peel, and sesame oil; lift with 2 forks to mix. Keep warm.

4. Drain basil and cilantro; blot dry. Cut leaves from stems, discarding stems. Place leaves in a blender or food processor with dried basil (if used), broth, and salad oil. Whirl until smooth. Spread on individual plates. Top with pasta and crab. Garnish with reserved sprigs. Makes 4 servings.

Per serving: 383 calories (29% fat, 52% carbohydrates, 19% protein), 13 g total fat (2 g saturated), 49 g carbohydrates, 19 g protein, 43 mg cholesterol, 474 mg sodium

CREAMY SHRIMP WITH LINGUINE

Preparation time: About 15 minutes

Cooking time: About 20 minutes

Cook shrimp in a creamy sauce of sun-dried tomatoes and serve on hot linguine for a showy main course.

- 3 tablespoons dried tomatoes packed in oil, drained (reserve oil) and chopped
- 1 clove garlic, minced or pressed
- 1 pound (455 g) large shrimp (31 to 35 per lb.), shelled and deveined
- 10 ounces (285 g) dried linguine
- ⅔ cup (160 ml) light cream
- ¼ cup (25 g) thinly sliced green onions
- 2 tablespoons chopped fresh basil or 1 teaspoon dried basil
- ⅛ teaspoon ground white pepper
- 2 teaspoons cornstarch mixed with ¾ cup (180 ml) nonfat milk
- 3 tablespoons dry vermouth (or to taste)
  Freshly grated Parmesan cheese
  Salt

1. Heat 1 teaspoon of the reserved oil from tomatoes in a wide nonstick frying pan over medium-high heat. Add garlic and shrimp. Cook, stirring often, just until shrimp are opaque in center; cut to test (about 6 minutes). Lift out and set aside, reserving any juices in pan.

2. Bring 12 cups (2.8 liters) water to a boil in a 5- to 6-quart (5- to 6-liter) pan over medium-high heat. Stir in pasta and cook just until tender to bite (8 to 10 minutes); or cook according to package directions. Meanwhile, combine cream, onions, basil, tomatoes, and white pepper with juices in frying pan. Bring to a boil over medium-high heat and cook, stirring, for 1 minute. Stir cornstarch mixture and add to pan. Return mixture to a boil and cook, stirring, just until slightly thickened. Remove from heat; stir in vermouth and shrimp.

3. Drain pasta well and arrange on individual plates. Top with shrimp mixture. Offer cheese and salt to add to taste. Makes 4 servings.

Per serving: 547 calories (29% fat, 47% carbohydrates, 24% protein), 17 g total fat (6 g saturated), 63 g carbohydrates, 31 g protein, 167 mg cholesterol, 188 mg sodium

Crab with Emerald Sauce (recipe above left) ▶

CRAB LASAGNE

Preparation time: About 30 minutes

Cooking time: About 1¾ hours

Try lasagne with crabmeat for an elegant casserole.

- 2¼ **pounds (1.02 kg) fennel, ends trimmed**
- 2 **large onions (about 1 lb./455 g *total*), thinly sliced**
- 12 **ounces (340 g) mushrooms, sliced**
- 2 **cups (470 ml) low-sodium chicken broth**
- 8 **ounces (230 g) dried lasagne**
- 2 **cups (470 ml) low-fat milk**
- ¼ **cup (60 ml) dry sherry**
- ¼ **cup (32 g) cornstarch mixed with ⅓ cup (80 ml) water**
- 8 **ounces/230 g (about 2 cups) shredded fontina cheese**
- ¾ **to 1 pound (340 to 455 g) cooked crabmeat**

1. Slice fennel thinly crosswise, reserving feathery tops. Mix fennel, onions, and mushrooms in a 12- by 14-inch (30- by 35.5-cm) baking pan. Bake in a 475°F (245°C) oven, stirring occasionally, until browned bits stick to pan bottom (about 45 minutes); do not scorch. To deglaze pan, add ½ cup (120 ml) of the broth, stirring to loosen browned bits. Continue to bake until browned bits form again (about 20 more minutes). Repeat deglazing step, adding ½ cup (120 ml) more broth, and bake until vegetables are well browned. Add ½ cup (120 ml) more broth, stirring to loosen browned bits. Keep warm.

2. Bring 12 cups (2.8 liters) water to a boil in a 5- to 6-quart (5- to 6-liter) pan over medium-high heat. Stir in pasta and cook just until tender to bite (8 to 10 minutes); or cook according to package directions. Drain well; blot dry.

3. Mince enough of the reserved fennel to make ¼ cup (60 ml). In a wide nonstick frying pan, combine minced fennel, milk, sherry, and remaining ½ cup (120 ml) broth. Bring to a boil over high heat. Stir cornstarch mixture and add to pan. Cook, stirring, until sauce comes to a boil. Remove from heat, add half the cheese, and stir until smooth. Keep hot.

4. Arrange a third of the pasta in a 9- by 13-inch (23- by 33-cm) baking pan. Spread with vegetables and half the sauce. Cover with a third more of the pasta, crab, and all but ½ cup (120 ml) of the sauce. Top with remaining pasta, sauce, and cheese. Bake in a 450°F (230°C) oven

until bubbling (about 10 minutes). Broil 4 to 6 inches (10 to 15 cm) below heat until browned (4 to 5 minutes). Let stand for 5 minutes. Makes 6 to 8 servings.

Per serving: 421 calories (29% fat, 42% carbohydrates, 29% protein), 13 g total fat (7 g saturated), 43 g carbohydrates, 30 g protein, 98 mg cholesterol, 593 mg sodium

SCALLOPS WITH ROTINI

Preparation time: About 10 minutes

Cooking time: About 20 minutes

There's a hint of heat in this quickly prepared entrée.

- 1 **pound/455 g (about 7 cups) dried rotini or other corkscrew-shaped pasta**
- 1½ **pounds (680 g) bay scallops, rinsed and drained**
- 1 **teaspoon paprika**
- ½ **teaspoon *each* dried basil, dried thyme, dried mustard, and ground white pepper**
- 2 **teaspoons salad oil**
- 1 **cup (240 ml) low-sodium chicken broth**
- 1½ **tablespoons cornstarch mixed with ⅓ cup (80 ml) water**
- ½ **cup (120 ml) reduced-fat or regular sour cream**

1. Bring 16 cups (3.8 liters) water to a boil in a 6- to 8-quart (6- to 8-liter) pan over medium-high heat. Stir in pasta and cook just until tender to bite (8 to 10 minutes); or cook according to package directions. Meanwhile, place scallops in a large bowl. Add paprika, basil, thyme, mustard, and white pepper. Mix until scallops are well coated. Heat oil in a wide nonstick frying pan over medium-high heat. Add scallops and cook, stirring often, just until opaque in center; cut to test (about 3 minutes). Lift out and set aside, reserving juices in pan.

2. Drain pasta well. Transfer to a platter and keep warm.

3. Increase heat to high and cook reserved juices until reduced to about ¼ cup (60 ml). Add broth and bring to a boil. Stir cornstarch mixture and add to broth. Bring to a boil again, stirring. Remove from heat and stir in sour cream and scallops. Spoon over pasta. Makes 6 servings.

Per serving: 444 calories (14% fat, 58% carbohydrates, 28% protein), 7 g total fat (2 g saturated), 63 g carbohydrates, 31 g protein, 44 mg cholesterol, 219 mg sodium

SMOKED SALMON WITH VODKA & BOW TIES

Preparation time: About 15 minutes

Cooking time: About 25 minutes

A vodka-infused sauce enhances bow-shaped pasta and silken smoked salmon.

- 12 ounces/340 g (about 6 cups) dried farfalle (about 1½-inch/3.5-cm size)
- 1 teaspoon olive oil
- 1 small shallot, thinly sliced
- 4 small pear-shaped (Roma-type) tomatoes (about 6 oz./170 g *total*), peeled, seeded, and chopped
- ⅔ cup (160 ml) half-and-half
- 3 tablespoons vodka
- 2 tablespoons chopped fresh dill or ½ teaspoon dried dill weed (or to taste)
  Pinch of ground nutmeg
- 4 to 6 ounces (115 to 170 g) sliced smoked salmon or lox, cut into bite-size strips
  Dill sprigs
  Ground white pepper

1. Bring 12 cups (2.8 liters) water to a boil in a 5- to 6-quart (5- to 6-liter) pan over medium-high heat. Stir in pasta and cook just until tender to bite (8 to 10 minutes); or cook according to package directions. Drain well and keep warm.

2. Heat oil in a wide nonstick frying pan over medium-low heat. Add shallot and cook, stirring often, until soft but not browned (about 3 minutes). Stir in tomatoes; cover and simmer for 5 minutes. Add half-and-half, vodka, chopped dill, and nutmeg. Increase heat to medium-high and bring to a boil. Cook, stirring often, for 1 minute.

3. Add pasta and mix thoroughly but gently. Remove from heat and stir in salmon. Transfer to a platter. Garnish with dill sprigs. Offer white pepper to add to taste. Makes 4 or 5 servings.

Per serving: 385 calories (24% fat, 59% carbohydrates, 17% protein), 10 g total fat (4 g saturated), 54 g carbohydrates, 15 g protein, 28 mg cholesterol, 243 mg sodium

ORECCHIETTE WITH SAKE-CLAM SAUCE

Preparation time: About 10 minutes

Cooking time: About 20 minutes

Round and rimmed, orecchiette may look like diminutive caps, but they translate as "little ears."

- 2 cans (about 6½ oz./185 g *each*) chopped clams
- ¾ cup (130 g) finely chopped onions
- 2 cloves garlic, minced or pressed
- 1 cup (240 ml) sake or dry vermouth
- 2 tablespoons capers, drained
- 8 ounces/230 g (about 2⅓ cups) dried orecchiette or other medium-size pasta shape
- ¼ cup (15 g) finely chopped parsley
- ¼ cup (20 g) freshly grated Parmesan cheese
- ⅛ teaspoon crushed red pepper flakes

1. Drain clams, reserving juice. Set clams aside.

2. Combine ½ cup (120 ml) of the clam juice, onions, garlic, and ¼ cup (60 ml) of the sake in a wide nonstick frying pan. Cook over high heat, stirring often, until about a quarter of the liquid remains (about 3 minutes). Add clams, capers, and remaining ¾ cup (180 ml) sake. Reduce heat and simmer, uncovered, for about 4 minutes. Remove from heat and keep warm.

3. Bring 8 cups (1.9 liters) water to a boil in a 4- to 5-quart (3.8- to 5-liter) pan over medium-high heat. Stir in pasta and cook just until tender to bite (8 to 10 minutes); or cook according to package directions. Drain well. Transfer to a wide serving bowl. Quickly add clam mixture and stir until most of the liquid is absorbed. Add parsley, cheese, and red pepper flakes. Mix thoroughly but gently. Makes 4 servings.

Per serving: 381 calories (10% fat, 62% carbohydrates, 28% protein), 3 g total fat (1 g saturated), 49 g carbohydrates, 22 g protein, 36 mg cholesterol, 266 mg sodium

Beef, Pork, Lamb & Veal

Eating light doesn't mean that you can't include meat in your diet. The secret is to use moderate amounts of lean beef, pork, lamb, and veal and pair them with low-fat pasta, which reduces the entrée's total fat content. Whether you try tempting Beef Mostaccioli, Asian-inspired Pork Tenderloin with Peanut Vermicelli, or succulent Veal Chops with Noodle Pudding, you're sure to appreciate the great taste and healthy approach of these pasta and meat combinations.

◀ *Beef-on-a-Stick with Saffron Couscous*
(recipe on page 68)

BEEF-ON-A-STICK WITH SAFFRON COUSCOUS

Pictured on page 66

Preparation time: About 15 minutes

Marinating time: At least 30 minutes

Cooking time: About 15 minutes

Tinged golden with saffron, couscous makes a fluffy bed for marinated beef kebabs.

- 1½ **pounds (680 g) lean boneless top sirloin steak (about 1 inch/2.5 cm thick), trimmed of fat**
- ½ **cup (120 ml) reduced-sodium soy sauce**
- 2 **tablespoons *each* honey and red wine vinegar**
- 1 **clove garlic, minced or pressed**
- ½ **teaspoon ground ginger**
- ¼ **teaspoon pepper**
- 1 **teaspoon olive oil**
- 1 **large onion (about 8 oz./230 g), chopped**
- 2 **cups (470 ml) nonfat milk**
- ¾ **cup (180 ml) low-sodium chicken broth**
  Large pinch of saffron threads or ⅛ teaspoon saffron powder (or to taste)
- 10 **ounces/285 g (about 1⅔ cups) dried couscous**
- ¼ **cup (20 g) freshly grated Parmesan cheese (or to taste)**
  Tomato wedges
  Italian parsley sprigs

1. Slice steak across grain into strips about ¼ inch (6 mm) thick and 4 inches (10 cm) long (for easier slicing, freeze steak for about 30 minutes before cutting). Place meat, soy sauce, honey, vinegar, garlic, ginger, pepper, and 2 tablespoons water in a large heavy-duty resealable plastic bag or large nonmetal bowl. Seal bag and rotate to coat meat (or turn meat in bowl and cover airtight). Refrigerate for at least 30 minutes or up to a day, turning (or stirring) occasionally. Meanwhile, soak 12 wooden skewers (8 to 10 inches/20 to 25 cm long) in hot water to cover for at least 30 minutes.

2. Lift meat from marinade and drain, reserving marinade. Weave 2 or 3 meat slices on each skewer so meat lies flat. Place in a lightly oiled broiler pan without a rack and set aside.

3. Heat oil in a 2- to 3-quart (1.9- to 2.8-liter) pan over medium-high heat. Add onion and cook, stirring often, until soft (about 5 minutes). Add milk, broth, and saffron; bring just to a boil. Stir in pasta; cover, remove from heat, and let stand until liquid is absorbed (about 5 minutes). Meanwhile, broil meat 3 to 4 inches (8 to 10 cm) below heat, basting with reserved marinade and turning as needed, until done to your liking; cut to test (about 5 minutes for medium-rare).

4. Fluff pasta with a fork, adding cheese. Spoon onto a platter and top with meat. Garnish with tomatoes and parsley. Makes 6 servings (2 skewers each).

Per serving: 435 calories (18% fat, 46% carbohydrates, 36% protein), 9 g total fat (3 g saturated), 49 g carbohydrates, 38 g protein, 80 mg cholesterol, 1,333 mg sodium

BEEF MOSTACCIOLI

Preparation time: About 15 minutes

Cooking time: About 45 minutes

Basil and fennel turn a simple pasta, beef, and tomato casserole into delicious family fare.

- 1 **pound (455 g) lean ground beef**
- 1 **large onion (about 8 oz./230 g), chopped**
- 3 **cloves garlic, minced or pressed**
- ¾ **teaspoon fennel seeds**
- 12 **ounces/340 g (about 4 cups) dried mostaccioli or penne**
- 2 **cans (about 15 oz./425 g *each*) tomato purée**
- 3 **tablespoons chopped fresh basil or 1 tablespoon dried basil**
- ¼ **cup (60 ml) dry red wine (or to taste)**
  Salt and pepper
- 2 **cups (about 8 oz./230 g) shredded part-skim mozzarella cheese**
  Basil sprigs (optional)

1. Crumble meat into a 4- to 5-quart (3.8- to 5-liter) pan. Add onion, garlic, fennel seeds, and 2 tablespoons water. Cook over medium-high heat, stirring often, until meat is well browned (about 15 minutes); if pan appears dry or mixture sticks to pan bottom, add more water, 1 tablespoon at a time. Meanwhile, bring 12 cups (2.8 liters) water to a boil in a 5- to 6-quart (5- to 6-liter) pan over medium-high heat. Stir in pasta and cook just until tender to bite (8 to 10 minutes); or cook according to package directions. Drain well and transfer to a large nonmetal bowl; keep warm.

2. Add tomato purée and chopped basil to meat mixture; reduce heat to medium and cook, stirring, until hot. Transfer to bowl with pasta. Add wine and mix thoroughly but gently. Season to taste with salt and pepper.

3. Spoon into a 2½- to 3-quart (2.4- to 2.8-liter) casserole. Cover tightly and bake in a 350°F (175°C) oven for 15 minutes. Uncover, sprinkle with cheese, and continue to bake until mixture is bubbly (about 15 more minutes). Garnish with basil sprigs, if desired. Makes 6 to 8 servings.

Per serving: 448 calories (25% fat, 48% carbohydrates, 27% protein), 13 g total fat (6 g saturated), 54 g carbohydrates, 30 g protein, 59 mg cholesterol, 688 mg sodium

CHILE BEEF STIR-FRY WITH SESAME GEMELLI

Preparation time: About 15 minutes

Marinating time: At least 30 minutes

Cooking time: About 15 minutes

An intriguing interplay of hot and cold sets this stir-fry apart from others.

- **1 teaspoon sesame seeds**
- **1 pound (455 g) lean boneless top sirloin steak (about 1 inch/2.5 cm thick), trimmed of fat**
- **1 jalapeño or other small hot chile, stemmed, seeded, and minced**
- **4 cloves garlic, minced or pressed**
- **3 tablespoons reduced-sodium soy sauce**
- **1½ teaspoons sugar**
- **¼ to ½ teaspoon ground red pepper (cayenne)**
- **10 ounces/285 g (about 3¼ cups) dried gemelli or rotini**
- **1 teaspoon salad oil**
- **½ cup (120 ml) seasoned rice vinegar; or ½ cup (120 ml) distilled white vinegar and 4 teaspoons sugar**
- **1 tablespoon Oriental sesame oil**

- **6 cups (330 g) bite-size pieces mixed greens, such as watercress, arugula, radicchio, butterhead lettuce, and red leaf lettuce, rinsed and crisped**
- **Salt and pepper**

1. Toast sesame seeds in a small nonstick frying pan over medium heat, shaking pan often, until golden (about 3 minutes). Remove from pan and set aside.

2. Slice steak across grain into strips about ⅛ inch (3 mm) thick and 3 inches (8 cm) long (for easier slicing, freeze steak for 30 minutes before cutting). Place meat, chile, garlic, soy sauce, sugar, and pepper in a large heavy-duty resealable plastic bag or large nonmetal bowl. Seal bag and rotate to coat meat (or turn meat in bowl and cover airtight). Refrigerate for at least 30 minutes or up to a day, turning (or stirring) occasionally.

3. Bring 12 cups (2.8 liters) water to a boil in a 5- to 6-quart (5- to 6-liter) pan over medium-high heat. Stir in pasta and cook just until tender to bite (8 to 10 minutes); or cook according to package directions. Meanwhile, heat salad oil in a wide nonstick frying pan over medium-high heat. Add steak and its juices and cook, stirring, until browned and done to your liking; cut to test (3 to 5 minutes).

4. Drain pasta and keep warm. In a large nonmetal serving bowl, stir together vinegar, sesame oil, and sesame seeds. Add greens, pasta, and meat and its juices; turn to coat. Offer salt and pepper to add to taste. Makes 4 or 5 servings.

Per serving: 509 calories (20% fat, 52% carbohydrates, 28% protein), 11 g total fat (3 g saturated), 65 g carbohydrates, 35 g protein, 69 mg cholesterol, 1,127 mg sodium

PORK TENDERLOIN WITH PEANUT VERMICELLI

Pictured on facing page

Preparation time: About 20 minutes

Cooking time: About 35 minutes

Peanuts, plum jam, hoisin, and peas star in this dish.

- 2 **pork tenderloins (about 12 oz./340 g *each*), trimmed of fat and silvery membrane**
- ¼ **cup (60 ml) hoisin sauce**
- 3 **tablespoons firmly packed brown sugar**
- 2 **tablespoons dry sherry**
- 2 **tablespoons reduced-sodium soy sauce**
- 1 **tablespoon lemon juice**
- 12 **ounces (340 g) dried vermicelli**
- ½ **cup (160 g) plum jam or plum butter**
- ¼ **cup (60 ml) seasoned rice vinegar; or ¼ cup (60 ml) distilled white vinegar and 2 teaspoons sugar**
- ¼ **cup (65 g) creamy peanut butter**
- 3 **tablespoons Oriental sesame oil**
- 2 **cloves garlic, minced or pressed**
- ⅛ **teaspoon ground ginger**
- ¼ **teaspoon crushed red pepper flakes**
- 1 **package (about 10 oz./285 g) frozen tiny peas, thawed**
- ⅓ **cup (15 g) cilantro**
- 2 **tablespoons chopped peanuts (optional)**
  Sliced kumquats (optional)

1. Place tenderloins on a rack in a 9- by 13-inch (23- by 33-cm) baking pan. In a bowl, stir together hoisin, brown sugar, sherry, 1 tablespoon of the soy sauce, and lemon juice. Brush over pork, reserving remaining mixture.

2. Roast pork in a 450°F (230°C) oven, brushing with remaining marinade, until a meat thermometer inserted in thickest part registers 155°F/68°C (20 to 30 minutes; after 15 minutes, check temperature every 5 minutes); if drippings begin to burn, add 4 to 6 tablespoons water, stirring to loosen browned bits. Meanwhile, bring 12 cups (2.8 liters) water to a boil in a 5- to 6-quart (5- to 6-liter) pan over medium-high heat. Stir in pasta and cook just until tender to bite (8 to 10 minutes); or cook according to package directions. Drain well and keep warm.

3. Transfer meat to a board, cover loosely, and let stand for 10 minutes. Skim and discard fat from pan drippings. Pour drippings and any juices on board into a small serving container; keep warm. Meanwhile, combine jam, vinegar, peanut butter, oil, garlic, ginger, red pepper flakes, and remaining 1 tablespoon soy sauce in 5- to 6-quart (5- to 6-liter) pan. Bring to a boil over medium heat and cook, whisking, just until smooth. Remove from heat and add pasta, peas, and cilantro. Lift with 2 forks to mix. Mound pasta on individual plates. Thinly slice meat across grain; arrange on pasta. Garnish with kumquats, if desired. Offer juices and, if desired, peanuts to add to taste. Makes 6 servings.

Per serving: 631 calories (25% fat, 51% carbohydrates, 24% protein), 18 g total fat (3 g saturated), 80 g carbohydrates, 37 g protein, 67 mg cholesterol, 919 mg sodium

PORK STEW WITH SPAETZLE

Preparation time: About 10 minutes

Cooking time: About 2 hours

Spaetzle is often paired with sauerkraut as in this stew.

- 1 **pound (455 g) boned pork shoulder or butt, trimmed of fat, cut into 1-inch (2.5-cm) cubes**
- 1 **can (about 1 lb./455 g) sauerkraut, drained**
- ¼ **cup (65 g) tomato paste**
- 3 **tablespoons paprika**
- 2 **tablespoons sugar**
- 1 **pound (455 g) carrots, cut diagonally ¼ inch (6 mm) thick**
- 10½ **ounces/300 g (about 2 cups) dried spaetzle or fettuccine**
- ¼ **cup (15 g) chopped parsley**
- ½ **teaspoon caraway seeds (or to taste)**

1. Place pork and ¼ cup (60 ml) water in a 5- to 6-quart (5- to 6-liter) pan. Cover and cook over medium-high heat for 10 minutes. Uncover, increase heat to high, and bring to a boil. Cook, stirring often, until liquid has evaporated and drippings are well browned.

2. Add sauerkraut, tomato paste, paprika, sugar, and 3 cups (710 ml) more water. Bring to a boil; reduce heat, cover, and simmer for 1 hour.

3. Stir in carrots. Cover and cook until pork is tender when pierced (about 30 more minutes). Meanwhile,

Pork Tenderloin with Peanut Vermicelli ▶ *(recipe above left)*

bring 12 cups (2.8 liters) water to a boil in a 5- to 6-quart (5- to 6-liter) pan over medium-high heat. Stir in pasta and cook just until tender to bite (about 10 minutes for spaetzle, 8 to 10 minutes for fettuccine); or cook according to package directions. Drain well. Stir in 2 tablespoons of the parsley and caraway seeds. Arrange pasta and stew on individual plates. Sprinkle with remaining parsley. Makes 4 to 6 servings.

Per serving: 454 calories (21% fat, 54% carbohydrates, 25% protein), 11 g total fat (3 g saturated), 63 g carbohydrates, 28 g protein, 117 mg cholesterol, 420 mg sodium

PENNE ALL'ARRABBIATA

Preparation time: About 10 minutes

Cooking time: About 50 minutes

A spicy tomato sauce flecked with ham enlivens penne.

- 1 tablespoon olive oil
- 6 ounces (170 g) cooked ham, chopped
- 1 large onion (about 8 oz./230 g), finely chopped
- ½ cup (65 g) finely chopped carrot
- ½ cup (60 g) finely chopped celery
- ½ teaspoon crushed red pepper flakes
- 1 can (about 28 oz./795 g) pear-shaped (Roma-type) tomatoes
- 1 pound/455 g (about 5 cups) dried penne or ziti
- ¼ cup (20 g) freshly grated Parmesan cheese

1. Heat oil in a 3- to 4-quart (2.8- to 3.8-liter) pan over medium-high heat. Add ham and cook, stirring often, until lightly browned (about 5 minutes). Stir in onion, carrot, celery, and red pepper flakes. Reduce heat to medium and cook, stirring often, until vegetables are soft (about 15 minutes).

2. Add tomatoes and their liquid. Cook, stirring often, until sauce is reduced to about 3½ cups/830 ml (25 to 30 minutes). Meanwhile, bring 16 cups (3.8 liters) water to a boil in a 6- to 8-quart (6- to 8-liter) pan. Stir in pasta and cook just until tender to bite (8 to 10 minutes); or cook according to package directions. Drain well. Combine with sauce and cheese in a large serving bowl. Mix thoroughly but gently. Makes 4 or 5 servings.

Per serving: 500 calories (17% fat, 64% carbohydrates, 19% protein), 9 g total fat (3 g saturated), 80 g carbohydrates, 24 g protein, 24 mg cholesterol, 882 mg sodium

SMOKED PORK CHOPS WITH CHEESE WHEELS

Preparation time: About 10 minutes

Cooking time: About 25 minutes

Ruote, wheel-shaped pasta, is enveloped in a mustard-sparked cheese sauce and served with pan-browned smoked pork chops.

- 4 smoked pork loin chops (about 1¼ lbs./ 565 g *total*), each about ¾ inch (2 cm) thick, trimmed of fat
- 8 ounces/230 g (about 4 cups) dried ruote or other medium-size pasta shape
- 1 tablespoon butter or margarine
- 1 large onion (about 8 oz./230 g), chopped
- 1 tablespoon all-purpose flour
- 1½ cups (360 ml) nonfat milk
- 1 tablespoon Dijon mustard
- ¼ teaspoon pepper
- 1 package (about 10 oz./285 g) frozen tiny peas
- 1 cup (about 4 oz./115 g) shredded Emmenthaler or Swiss cheese

1. Place pork chops in a wide nonstick frying pan and cook over medium-high heat, turning as needed, until browned on both sides (about 10 minutes). Transfer to a platter and keep warm. Discard any pan drippings.

2. Bring 8 cups (1.9 liters) water to a boil in a 4- to 5-quart (3.8- to 5-liter) pan over medium-high heat. Stir in pasta and cook just until tender to bite (8 to 10 minutes); or cook according to package directions. Meanwhile, melt butter in frying pan over medium-high heat. Add onion and cook, stirring often, until soft (about 5 minutes). Stir in flour and remove from heat. Add milk, mustard, and pepper; mix until blended.

3. Stir peas into pasta and water; drain and set aside. Return sauce to medium-high heat and cook, stirring, until mixture comes to a boil. Add cheese and stir until melted. Remove from heat and add pasta mixture. Mix thoroughly but gently. Spoon alongside meat. Makes 4 servings.

Per serving: 594 calories (27% fat, 43% carbohydrates, 30% protein), 18 g total fat (9 g saturated), 64 g carbohydrates, 43 g protein, 86 mg cholesterol, 1,889 mg sodium

Lamb Chops with Cherries & Orecchiette

Preparation time: About 15 minutes

Cooking time: About 15 minutes

When cherries are in season, use them to make a delicious tart-sweet sauce for lamb rib chops.

- 8 lamb rib chops (about 2 lbs./905 g *total*), each about 1 inch (2.5 cm) thick, trimmed of fat
- 12 ounces/340 g (about 3½ cups) dried orecchiette or other medium-size pasta shape
- ⅓ cup (80 ml) seasoned rice vinegar; or ⅓ cup (80 ml) distilled white vinegar and 3 teaspoons sugar
- 1 tablespoon *each* chopped cilantro and chopped parsley
- 1 to 2 cloves garlic, minced or pressed
- ½ teaspoon ground coriander
- ¾ cup (225 g) currant jelly
- ½ cup (120 ml) raspberry vinegar
- ¼ cup (60 ml) orange juice
- 1 tablespoon chopped fresh tarragon or ¾ teaspoon dried tarragon
- 1½ cups (220 g) pitted dark sweet cherries

1. Place chops on lightly oiled rack of a broiler pan. Broil about 6 inches (15 cm) below heat, turning once, until done to your liking; cut to test (8 to 10 minutes). Meanwhile, bring 12 cups (2.8 liters) water to a boil in a 5- to 6-quart (5- to 6-liter) pan over medium-high heat. Stir in pasta and cook just until tender to bite (8 to 10 minutes); or cook according to package directions. Drain well. Transfer to a large nonmetal bowl and add rice vinegar, cilantro, parsley, garlic, and coriander; mix thoroughly but gently. Keep warm.

2. Combine jelly, raspberry vinegar, orange juice, and tarragon in a 1½- to 2-quart (1.4- to 1.9-liter) pan. Cook over medium heat, whisking, until smoothly blended. Add cherries and cook, stirring gently, just until warm. Remove from heat.

3. Spoon pasta onto individual plates. Arrange lamb chops alongside and top with fruit sauce. Makes 4 servings.

Per serving: 709 calories (14% fat, 68% carbohydrates, 18% protein), 11 g total fat (4 g saturated), 120 g carbohydrates, 32 g protein, 66 mg cholesterol, 481 mg sodium

Roast Lamb with Fettuccine Alfredo

Preparation time: About 25 minutes

Cooking time: About 50 minutes

Inspired by the classic Italian dish, ultra-lean fettuccine Alfredo is a perfect accompaniment to herb-seasoned roast lamb.

- 2 tablespoons *each* chopped parsley and honey
- 2 teaspoons Dijon mustard
- 1 teaspoon chopped fresh thyme or ½ teaspoon dried thyme
- 1 teaspoon chopped fresh rosemary or ¼ teaspoon crumbled dried rosemary
- 1 teaspoon chopped fresh sage or ½ teaspoon dried rubbed sage
- 1 teaspoon grated lemon peel
- 1 clove garlic, minced or pressed
- 1 boned lamb loin (about 1½ lbs./680 g), rolled and tied
- 2 cups (470 ml) nonfat milk
- ⅔ cup (160 ml) half-and-half
- 1 pound (455 g) dried fettuccine
- ⅓ cup (30 g) freshly grated Parmesan cheese
  Salt
  Pinch of ground nutmeg
- 1 or 2 lemons, cut into wedges

1. Mix parsley, honey, mustard, thyme, rosemary, sage, lemon peel, and garlic in a small bowl. Set aside.

2. Place lamb on a rack in a 9- by 13-inch (23- by 33-cm) pan. Roast in a 475°F (245°C) oven for 20 minutes; if drippings begin to burn, add 4 to 6 tablespoons water, stirring to loosen browned bits. Remove from oven, brush meat with honey mixture, and continue to roast until a meat thermometer inserted in thickest part registers 140°F (60°C) for rare (15 to 20 more minutes); if roast browns too quickly, drape with foil. Meanwhile, combine milk and half-and-half in a 1½- to 2-quart (1.4- to 1.9-liter) pan. Bring just to a boil over medium heat; reduce heat and simmer gently, stirring often, until reduced to about 2 cups/470 ml (about 30 minutes). Remove from heat and keep warm.

3. Transfer meat to a board, cover loosely, and let stand for 10 minutes. Skim and discard fat from pan drippings

and pour into a small serving container; keep warm. Meanwhile, bring 16 cups (3.8 liters) water to a boil in a 6- to 8-quart (6- to 8-liter) pan over medium-high heat. Stir in pasta and cook just until tender to bite (8 to 10 minutes); or cook according to package directions. Drain well.

4. Combine pasta, milk mixture, and cheese in a wide nonmetal bowl. Mix thoroughly but gently. Cover tightly and let stand for 5 minutes. Season to taste with salt and mix again. Cover and let stand for 5 more minutes. Meanwhile, remove and discard strings from meat; slice thinly. Add any juices on platter to pan drippings. Place meat on individual plates. Mound pasta alongside and sprinkle with nutmeg. Garnish with lemon wedges. Offer juices to add to taste. Makes 6 servings.

Per serving: 604 calories (29% fat, 44% carbohydrates, 27% protein), 19 g total fat (9 g saturated), 66 g carbohydrates, 40 g protein, 172 mg cholesterol, 328 mg sodium

ITALIAN SAUSAGE LASAGNE

Pictured on facing page

Preparation time: About 25 minutes

Cooking time: About 2 hours

Because this slimmed-down lasagne is not layered like traditional lasagne, it goes together quickly.

    Low-fat Italian Sausage (page 19)

  3 **large onions (about 1½ lbs./680 g *total*), chopped**

  2 **large stalks celery (about 8 oz./230 g *total*), chopped**

  2 **medium-size carrots (about 6 oz./170 g *total*), chopped**

  5 **cups (1.2 liters) beef broth**

  1 **can (about 6 oz./170 g) tomato paste**

1½ **teaspoons dried basil**

½ **teaspoon dried rosemary**

¼ **teaspoon ground nutmeg**

12 **ounces (340 g) dried lasagne**

  3 **tablespoons cornstarch**

1½ **cups (360 ml) nonfat milk**

  2 **cups (about 8 oz./230 g) shredded fontina cheese**

½ **cup (40 g) freshly grated Parmesan cheese**

1. Prepare Low-fat Italian Sausage; refrigerate, covered.

2. Combine onions, celery, carrots, and 1½ cups (360 ml) of the broth in a 5- to 6-quart (5- to 6-liter) pan (preferably nonstick). Bring to a boil over high heat and cook, stirring occasionally, until liquid has evaporated and vegetables begin to brown (12 to 15 minutes). To deglaze pan, add ¼ cup (60 ml) water, stirring to loosen browned bits. Continue to cook, stirring often, until mixture begins to brown again. Repeat deglazing step, adding ¼ cup (60 ml) more water each time, until mixture is richly browned.

3. Crumble sausage into pan; add ½ cup (120 ml) more water. Cook, stirring occasionally, until liquid has evaporated and meat begins to brown (about 10 minutes). Add ⅓ cup (80 ml) more water and cook, stirring, until meat is browned (2 to 4 more minutes). Reduce heat to medium-low and add 2½ cups (590 ml) more broth, stirring to loosen browned bits. Add tomato paste, basil, rosemary, and nutmeg. Bring to a boil; reduce heat, cover, and simmer, stirring occasionally, until flavors have blended (about 20 minutes). Meanwhile, bring 12 cups (2.8 liters) water to a boil in a 5- to 6-quart (5- to 6-liter) pan over medium-high heat. Stir in pasta and cook just until barely tender to bite (about 8 minutes). Drain well and keep warm.

4. Blend remaining 1 cup (240 ml) broth with cornstarch and milk until smooth. Add to meat mixture. Cook over medium-high heat, stirring, until bubbling and thickened. Stir in 1 cup (115 g) of the fontina; remove from heat. Gently stir in pasta. Transfer to a shallow 3-quart (2.8-liter) baking dish; swirl pasta. Sprinkle with Parmesan and remaining 1 cup (115 g) fontina. (At this point, you may cool, cover, and refrigerate for up to a day.)

5. Bake in a 375°F (190°C) oven until bubbling (about 30 minutes; 35 to 40 minutes if chilled). Makes 8 servings.

Per serving: 481 calories (28% fat, 45% carbohydrates, 27% protein), 15 g total fat (8 g saturated), 54 g carbohydrates, 33 g protein, 76 mg cholesterol, 1,116 mg sodium

◄ *Italian Sausage Lasagne (recipe above)*

When you don't have the time to make your own homemade pasta, purchased egg roll (spring roll), potsticker (gyoza), and won ton wrappers can help you turn out pasta specialties that are still impressive and delicious. In general, the purchased wrappers are thinner than freshly made pasta, so be sure to handle them gently when working with them.

Because these Asian wrappers are generous in size, they hold more filling than their classic counterparts, making rather large versions of each pasta specialty. To cut the skins into rounds for tortellini, use a 3- to 3¼-inch (8- to 8.25-cm) cookie cutter.

Look for the wrappers in the produce or refrigerated dairy section of your supermarket or in an Asian market.

CANDY-WRAP PASTA WITH CHEESE & BLACK BEAN SAUCE

Preparation time: About 30 minutes

Cooking time: About 20 minutes

8 ounces (230 g) *each* **feta cheese** and **part-skim ricotta cheese**

½ cup (20 g) firmly packed **cilantro**

2 tablespoons *each* freshly grated **Parmesan cheese** and **milk**

18 **egg roll (spring roll) wrappers**

2 tablespoons **all-purpose flour** mixed with ¼ cup (60 ml) **water**

Black Bean Sauce (recipe follows)

1. Combine feta, ricotta, ⅓ cup (15 g) of the cilantro, Parmesan, and milk in a food processor or blender. Whirl until smooth.

2. Lay a wrapper flat, keeping remaining wrappers covered, and place 1 heaping tablespoon of the cheese mixture in center along edge of one side (a narrow side if rectangular). Pat mixture into a log about ¾ inch by 1½ inches (2 by 3.5 cm). Stir flour mixture. With your finger, lightly rub mixture along each side of filling to opposite edge of wrapper. Also rub mixture along edge opposite filling.

3. Roll wrapper up gently, starting at edge with filling; press edge to seal. Firmly squeeze dough together at ends of filling where paste is painted (pasta should look like a piece of candy twisted in paper). Lay on a lightly floured large baking sheet and cover with plastic wrap. Repeat to use all filling, arranging pasta in a single layer; use 2 baking sheets, if necessary. (At this point, you may refrigerate for up to 4 hours.)

4. Prepare Black Bean Sauce.

5. Chop remaining cilantro; set aside.

6. Pour water into a wide frying pan to a depth of 2 inches (5 cm). Bring to a boil over high heat. Reduce heat to a gentle boil. Add pasta, half at a time, and cook just until tender to bite (2 to 3 minutes); if skins stick to each other or to pan bottom, stir gently to loosen. Drain well and keep warm.

7. Spoon sauce onto individual plates. Top with pasta. Sprinkle with cilantro. Makes 6 servings.

BLACK BEAN SAUCE. Combine 1 tablespoon **butter** or margarine and 1 small **onion** (about 4 oz./115 g), chopped, in a wide nonstick frying pan. Cook over medium heat, stirring often, until onion is lightly browned (about 8 minutes). Transfer to a food processor or blender with 1 can (about 15 oz./425 g) **black beans** and their liquid and 1 cup (240 ml) **low-sodium chicken broth.** Whirl until smooth. Season to taste with **salt** and **pepper.**

Pour sauce into a 1½- to 2-quart (1.4- to 1.9-liter) pan. Cook over medium heat, stirring, until hot. Remove from heat and keep warm.

Per serving: 547 calories (26% fat, 55% carbohydrates, 19% protein), 16 g total fat (10 g saturated), 75 g carbohydrates, 25 g protein, 62 mg cholesterol, 1,360 mg sodium

CHICKEN TORTELLINI WITH CREAM SAUCE

Preparation time: About 1 hour

Cooking time: About 1¼ hours

Chicken-Prosciutto Filling (recipe follows)

6 dozen (12 to 14 oz./340 to 400 g) potsticker (gyoza) or won ton skins, cut into 3- to 3¼-inch (8- to 8.25-cm) rounds

1 large egg white

Lean Cream Sauce (recipe follows)

½ cup (40 g) freshly grated Parmesan cheese

1. Prepare Chicken-Prosciutto Filling. Lay a wrapper flat, keeping remaining wrappers covered, and place about 1 teaspoon of the filling in center. Moisten edges with egg white, fold over filling, and press to seal. Bring pointed ends together, overlapping; moisten ends with egg white and press to seal. Lay on a lightly floured large baking sheet and cover with plastic wrap. Repeat to use all filling, arranging pasta in

a single layer; use 2 baking sheets, if necessary. (At this point, you may refrigerate for up to 4 hours.)

2. Prepare Lean Cream Sauce.

3. Bring 12 cups (2.8 liters) water to a boil in each of two 5- to 6-quart (5- to 6-liter) pans over medium-high heat. Reduce heat to a gentle boil. Carefully lower half the pasta into each pan and cook just until tender to bite (4 to 5 minutes); if tortellini stick to each other or to pan bottom, stir gently to loosen. Drain well.

4. Pour a third of the sauce into a large serving bowl. Add pasta and top with remaining sauce. Sprinkle with cheese. Makes 6 to 8 servings.

CHICKEN-PROSCIUTTO FILLING.
Finely chop 4 ounces (115 g) thinly sliced **prosciutto.** Bone and skin a 1-pound (455-g) **chicken breast;** cut meat into ½-inch (1-cm) pieces. Set aside.

Combine 1 extra-large **onion** (about 10 oz./285 g), chopped, and 1 cup (240 ml) **low-sodium chicken broth** in a wide nonstick frying pan. Bring to a boil over high heat and

cook, stirring occasionally, until liquid has evaporated and onion begins to brown (about 12 minutes). To deglaze pan, add ⅓ cup (80 ml) **water,** stirring to loosen browned bits. Continue to cook, stirring often, until liquid has evaporated and onion begins to brown again. Repeat deglazing step, adding ⅓ cup (80 ml) more **water** each time, until onion is richly browned.

Add chicken and prosciutto. Cook, stirring often, until chicken is no longer pink in center; cut to test (about 3 minutes).

Whirl mixture in a food processor until coarsely ground; or finely chop. Mix with 1 large **egg white,** ¼ cup (20 g) freshly grated **Parmesan cheese,** 2 tablespoons *each* **all-purpose flour** and more **low-sodium chicken broth,** and ¼ teaspoon **ground nutmeg.** Season to taste with **salt** and **pepper.**

LEAN CREAM SAUCE. Combine
1 extra-large **onion** (about 10 oz./ 285 g), finely chopped, and 1 cup (240 ml) **low-sodium chicken broth** in a wide nonstick frying pan. Bring to a boil over high heat and cook, stirring occasionally, until liquid has evaporated and onion begins to brown (about 12 minutes). To deglaze pan, add ⅓ cup (80 ml) **water,** stirring to loosen browned bits. Continue to cook, stirring often, until liquid has evaporated and onion begins to brown again. Repeat deglazing step, adding ⅓ cup (80 ml) more **water** each time, until onion is richly browned.

Add 1 tablespoon **cornstarch,** ¼ teaspoon **ground nutmeg,** 2 cups (470 ml) **low-fat milk,** and ½ cup (120 ml) more **low-sodium chicken broth.** Bring just to a boil, stirring. Remove from heat and keep warm.

Per serving: 347 calories (19% fat, 50% carbohydrates, 31% protein), 7 g total fat (3 g saturated), 43 g carbohydrates, 27 g protein, 51 mg cholesterol, 822 mg sodium

Lamb Kebabs with Orzo

Preparation time: About 35 minutes

Cooking time: 20 to 25 minutes

Curry accents the lamb and onion skewers that rest atop creamy orzo studded with olives.

- 1 pound (455 g) boneless lean lamb, trimmed of fat, cut into 1-inch (2.5-cm) cubes
- 10 ounces (285 g) small onions (about 1-inch/ 2.5-cm diameter)
- 2½ teaspoons curry powder
- 2 cups (470 ml) nonfat milk
- 1½ cups (360 ml) low-sodium chicken broth
- 10 ounces/285 g (about 1⅔ cups) dried orzo or other rice-shaped pasta
- 1 tablespoon chopped fresh oregano or 1 teaspoon dried oregano
- ¼ cup (35 g) pitted black olives, cut into wedges
- 3 tablespoons dry white wine (or to taste)
- 2 tablespoons chopped parsley
- ¼ cup (20 g) freshly grated Parmesan cheese
  Salt and pepper

1. Soak 8 wooden skewers (8 to 10 inches/20 to 25 cm long) in hot water to cover for at least 30 minutes.

2. Combine lamb, onions, and curry powder in a large bowl; turn to coat. Alternately thread lamb and onions onto skewers. Place on lightly oiled rack of a broiler pan. Set aside briefly.

3. Combine milk and broth in a 4- to 5-quart (3.8- to 5-liter) pan. Bring just to a boil over medium heat. Stir in pasta and oregano. Reduce heat, cover, and simmer, stirring occasionally, until most of the liquid is absorbed (15 to 20 minutes); do not scorch. Meanwhile, broil meat and onions 3 to 4 inches (8 to 10 cm) below heat, turning as needed, until meat is browned and done to your liking; cut to test (8 to 10 minutes).

4. Add olives, wine, parsley, and cheese to pasta. Stir well. Mound on individual plates and top with skewers. Offer salt and pepper to add to taste. Makes 4 servings (2 skewers each).

Per serving: 571 calories (21% fat, 48% carbohydrates, 31% protein), 13 g total fat (5 g saturated), 67 g carbohydrates, 43 g protein, 87 mg cholesterol, 331 mg sodium

Lamb with Fruited Couscous

Preparation time: About 10 minutes

Cooking time: About 2 hours

Apricot wine and dried apricots flavor fluffy couscous with lamb.

- 1 tablespoon olive oil
- 1 pound (455 g) boned leg of lamb, trimmed of fat, cut into 1-inch (2.5-cm) cubes
- 1 large onion (about 8 oz./230 g), chopped
- 1½ teaspoons ground coriander
- 1 teaspoon ground ginger
- ½ teaspoon ground cumin
- ¼ teaspoon ground allspice
- 1 cinnamon stick (about 3 in./8 cm long)
- 2 cups (470 ml) low-sodium chicken broth
- ¼ cup (60 ml) apricot or orange muscat dessert wine
- 1 cup (about 6 oz./170 g) dried apricots
- 10 ounces/285 g (about 1⅔ cups) dried couscous

1. Heat oil in a 5- to 6-quart (5- to 6-liter) pan over medium-high heat. Add lamb and cook, turning often, until well browned (about 8 minutes). Lift out and set aside.

2. Add onion to pan and cook, stirring often, until soft (about 5 minutes). Add coriander, ginger, cumin, allspice, cinnamon stick, broth, and lamb. Bring to a boil; reduce heat, cover, and simmer until lamb is tender when pierced (about 1½ hours). Discard cinnamon stick. (At this point, you may cool, cover, and refrigerate for up to a day; discard fat and reheat to continue.)

3. Lift out lamb and place on a platter; keep warm. Skim off and discard fat from pan drippings (if not already done). Measure drippings. If less than 2⅓ cups (550 ml), add water and return to pan; if more, boil over high heat until reduced to 2⅓ cups (550 ml). Add wine and apricots; bring to a boil. Stir in pasta; cover, remove from heat, and let stand until liquid is absorbed (about 5 minutes). Fluff with a fork.

4. Mound pasta beside lamb. Makes 4 servings.

Per serving: 606 calories (15% fat, 61% carbohydrates, 24% protein), 10 g total fat (3 g saturated), 89 g carbohydrates, 36 g protein, 73 mg cholesterol, 112 mg sodium

Veal Chops with Noodle Pudding (recipe on page 80) ▶

VEAL CHOPS WITH NOODLE PUDDING

Pictured on page 79

Preparation time: About 15 minutes

Cooking time: About 3¼ hours

Moist and rich noodle pudding enhances veal chops.

- 8 **large veal loin chops (about 4 lbs./1.8 kg *total*), trimmed of fat**
  About 4 tablespoons all-purpose flour
- 2 **teaspoons olive oil**
- 16 **sage leaves**
- 1½ **cups (360 ml) dry white wine**
  Noodle Pudding (page 92)
- 2 **teaspoons brown sugar (or to taste)**
- 2 **tablespoons *each* minced parsley and finely chopped green onion**
- 4 **teaspoons white wine vinegar (or to taste)**
  Sage sprigs

1. Coat chops lightly with flour. Heat oil in a wide non-stick frying pan over medium heat. Add sage leaves. Cook, stirring, until darker in color (about 2 minutes). With a slotted spoon, remove from pan and set aside. Add chops, half at a time, and cook, turning as needed, until browned on both sides (about 6 minutes). Place in a lightly oiled 12- by 17-inch (30- by 43-cm) roasting pan, overlapping chops as little as possible. Top with sage leaves. Pour in wine. Cover tightly and bake in a 375°F (190°C) oven until tender when pierced and slightly pink in center; cut to test (about 2 hours). Meanwhile, prepare Noodle Pudding; keep warm.

2. Lift out chops and keep warm. Skim and discard fat from pan drippings and measure. If less than 1 cup (240 ml), add water and bring to a boil in a 1- to 1½-quart (950-ml to 1.4-liter) pan over high heat; if more, pour drippings into pan and boil until reduced to 1 cup (240 ml). Add sugar and cook, stirring, until melted; remove from heat. Stir in parsley, onion, and vinegar.

3. Arrange chops and pudding on individual plates. Drizzle gravy over chops. Garnish with sage sprigs. Makes 8 servings.

Per serving: 475 calories (26% fat, 44% carbohydrates, 30% protein), 13 g total fat (5 g saturated), 50 g carbohydrates, 33 g protein, 138 mg cholesterol, 313 mg sodium

BRAISED VEAL WITH ESCAROLE & FRESH PASTA

Preparation time: About 15 minutes

Cooking time: About 1⅓ hours

If desired, substitute boneless veal shoulder for the roast.

- 14 **to 16 ounces (400 to 455 g) Egg Pasta or Food Processor Pasta (pages 20–21), cut for thin noodles, or purchased fresh fettuccine**
- 2 **tablespoons olive oil**
- 2 **pounds (905 g) veal tip roast, trimmed of fat, cut into 1-inch (2.5-cm) cubes**
- 2 **ounces (55 g) thinly sliced prosciutto, shredded**
- 1 **large onion (about 8 oz./230 g), finely chopped**
- 1 **large carrot (about 4 oz./115 g), finely chopped**
- 1 **cup (240 ml) dry white wine**
- 18 **cups lightly packed shredded escarole (about 1½ lbs./680 g)**
- 4 **teaspoons cornstarch mixed with ½ cup (120 ml) water**

1. Prepare Egg Pasta. Cover and refrigerate.

2. Heat 1 tablespoon of the oil in a 5- to 6-quart (5- to 6-liter) pan (preferably nonstick) over medium-high heat. Add half the veal and cook, turning often, until browned (about 5 minutes); remove from pan. Repeat with remaining oil and veal. Set aside.

3. Add prosciutto, onion, and carrot to pan. Cook, stirring often, until soft (about 5 minutes). Return veal to pan. Add wine and 1 cup (240 ml) water. Bring to a boil; reduce heat, cover, and simmer, stirring occasionally, until veal is tender when pierced (about 1 hour). Meanwhile, bring 16 cups (3.8 liters) water to a boil in a 6- to 8-quart (6- to 8-liter) pan. Stir in pasta and cook just until tender to bite (1 to 3 minutes; or according to package directions). Drain well and transfer to a deep platter; keep warm.

4. Add escarole to veal, a portion at a time if needed, and cook, stirring, until wilted (about 3 minutes). Stir cornstarch mixture and add to veal. Increase heat to high and cook, stirring, until mixture comes to a boil. Spoon over pasta. Makes 6 servings.

Per serving: 454 calories (25% fat, 38% carbohydrates, 37% protein), 12 g total fat (3 g saturated), 43 g carbohydrates, 42 g protein, 198 mg cholesterol, 352 mg sodium

LASAGNE PARTY

As any cook knows, it takes time to put together a traditional lasagne, with its layers of pasta, sauce, and cheeses. For a fun—and more relaxing—way to serve lasagne, let your guests do the work. Each person simply layers ingredients from the lasagne buffet—pasta, vegetables, cheeses, tomato sauce—on a plate.

The lasagne party is ideal for informal occasions when guests show up over a period of time. There's no baking of the lasagne, but you do need to keep the ingredients hot on electric warming trays, over hot water in chafing dishes, or in an oven at the lowest setting. The cooked pasta holds best unheated. To reheat the pasta, have a large pan of simmering water on the range or on a portable burner. Dunk the pasta in the water for about 30 seconds or until hot. Use a slotted spoon or tongs to retrieve it.

If you like, add cooked meat, other vegetables, and freshly grated Parmesan cheese to the buffet table.

LASAGNE BUFFET

Preparation time: About 30 minutes

Cooking time: About 1½ hours

- 16 large carrots (about 4 lbs./ 1.8 kg total), thinly sliced
- 4 large red bell peppers (about 2 lbs./905 g total), seeded and cut into thin strips
- 4 large onions (about 2 lbs./ 905 g total), thinly sliced
- 1½ pounds (680 g) mushrooms, thinly sliced
- ⅓ cup (80 ml) balsamic vinegar
- 4½ teaspoons olive oil or salad oil
  Herbed Tomato Sauce (recipe follows)

- 1½ cups (360 ml) low-sodium chicken broth
- 3 containers (about 15 oz./425 g each) part-skim ricotta cheese
- 12 ounces (340 g) jack or mozzarella cheese, shredded
- 1 cup (about 4 oz./115 g) freshly grated Parmesan cheese
- 2 pounds (905 g) dried lasagne, broken into 4- to 5-inch (10- to 12.5-cm) lengths

1. Place carrots, bell peppers, onions, mushrooms, vinegar, and oil in two 10- by 15-inch (25- by 38-cm) pans, dividing evenly. Mix well. Roast in a 450°F (230°C) oven, stirring often, until vegetables are browned and browned bits stick to pan (60 to 70 minutes; do not scorch); if using one oven, switch pan positions every 20 minutes. Meanwhile, prepare Herbed Tomato Sauce.

2. Remove vegetables from oven and add ½ cup (120 ml) of the broth to each pan, stirring to loosen browned bits. Continue to roast, stirring often, until liquid has evaporated (about 15 more minutes). Transfer vegetables to a serving bowl and keep warm.

3. Combine ricotta, jack, Parmesan, and remaining ½ cup (120 ml)

broth in a shallow 2- to 2½-quart (1.9- to 2.4-liter) casserole. Cover and bake in a 300°F (150°C) oven until warm (about 25 minutes). Meanwhile, half-fill a 10- to 12-quart (10- to 12-liter) pan with water. Bring to a boil over medium-high heat. Stir in pasta and cook just until tender to bite (12 to 15 minutes); or cook according to package directions. Drain, immerse in cold water until cool, and drain again. Transfer to a serving bowl.

4. Set out vegetables, sauce, and cheeses; keep warm. Reheat pasta as directed at left. Makes 20 servings.

Per serving: 434 calories (29% fat, 50% carbohydrates, 21% protein), 14 g total fat (8 g saturated), 55 g carbohydrates, 22 g protein, 43 mg cholesterol, 327 mg sodium

HERBED TOMATO SAUCE. In a 5- to 6-quart (5- to 6-liter) pan, combine 4 cans (about 28 oz./795 g each) **pear-shaped (Roma-type) tomatoes** (break up with a spoon) and their liquid; 1 can (about 12 oz./340 g) **tomato paste**; 1 cup (240 ml) **dry red wine**; ¼ cup (10 g) finely chopped **fresh basil** or 2 tablespoons dried basil; 3 cloves **garlic**, minced or pressed; 1 tablespoon finely chopped **fresh rosemary** or 1 teaspoon dried rosemary; and 1 tablespoon finely chopped **fresh oregano** or 2 teaspoons dried oregano.

Bring to a boil over high heat; reduce heat and simmer, stirring occasionally, until reduced to about 12 cups/2.8 liters (about 45 minutes). Transfer to a serving bowl and keep warm. Makes about 12 cups (2.8 liters).

Per ½ cup (120 ml): 41 calories (8% fat, 76% carbohydrates, 16% protein), 0.5 g total fat (0.1 g saturated), 9 g carbohydrates, 2 g protein, 0 mg cholesterol, 328 mg sodium

MEATLESS MAIN DISHES

On the lookout for main-course dishes that offer a change of pace from the traditional meat and fish? Here's a selection of recipes that combine pasta and vegetables with legumes, cheese, or tofu. The result? Tasty, good-for-you dishes sparked by the creative use of vinegars, soy sauce, herbs, and spices. Serve sweet-spicy Thai Tofu & Tagliatelle, lightened-up Macaroni & Cheese, or zesty Bucatini & Black Beans, and see for yourself just how delicious and balanced meals made without meat can be.

◄ *Capellini with Roasted Tomatoes & White Beans*
  (recipe on page 84)

CAPELLINI WITH ROASTED TOMATOES & WHITE BEANS

Pictured on page 82

Preparation time: About 15 minutes

Cooking time: About 1¼ hours

As the vegetables for this pasta dish brown slowly in the oven, they caramelize, giving a rich, sweet flavor.

- 1 **medium-size red onion (about 8 oz./230 g), cut into ¾-inch (2-cm) chunks**
- 1 **tablespoon olive oil**
- 6 **tablespoons (90 ml) balsamic vinegar**
- 14 **medium-size pear-shaped (Roma-type) tomatoes (about 1¾ lbs./795 g *total*), halved lengthwise**
    Salt
- 8 **ounces (230 g) dried capellini**
- 2 **cans (about 15 oz./425 g *each*) cannellini (white kidney beans)**
- 3 **tablespoons chopped fresh thyme or 1 tablespoon dried thyme**
- 3 **tablespoons chopped fresh basil or 1 tablespoon dried basil**
    Thyme sprigs

1. Mix onion, 1 teaspoon of the oil, and 2 tablespoons of the vinegar in a lightly oiled square 8-inch (20-cm) baking pan. Arrange tomatoes, cut sides up, in a lightly oiled 9- by 13-inch (23- by 33-cm) baking pan; rub with remaining 2 teaspoons oil and season to taste with salt.

2. Bake onion and tomatoes in a 475°F (245°C) oven, switching pan positions halfway through baking, until edges are well browned (40 to 50 minutes for onion, about 1 hour and 10 minutes for tomatoes); if drippings begin to burn, add 4 to 6 tablespoons water to each pan, stirring to loosen browned bits. Meanwhile, bring 8 cups (1.9 liters) water to a boil in a 4- to 5-quart (3.8- to 5-liter) pan over medium-high heat. Stir in pasta and cook just until tender to bite (about 4 minutes); or cook according to package directions.

3. Drain pasta well and keep warm. Pour beans and their liquid into pan. Add chopped thyme (or dried thyme and dried basil, if used). Bring to a boil; reduce heat and simmer, stirring often, for 3 minutes. Add pasta; lift with 2 forks to mix. Remove from heat; keep warm.

4. Chop 10 of the tomato halves. Add to pasta with chopped basil (if used), onion, and remaining ¼ cup (60 ml) vinegar. Transfer pasta to a wide, shallow serving bowl. Arrange remaining tomato halves around edge. Garnish with thyme sprigs. Makes 4 to 6 servings.

Per serving: 402 calories (12% fat, 71% carbohydrates, 17% protein), 6 g total fat (0.8 g saturated), 74 g carbohydrates, 17 g protein, 0 mg cholesterol, 618 mg sodium

TOFU-SPINACH MANICOTTI

Preparation time: About 25 minutes

Cooking time: About 1½ hours

Spinach and tofu make a lean filling for baked manicotti.

- 2 **tablespoons olive oil**
- 1 **medium-size onion (about 6 oz./170 g), chopped**
- 3 **medium-size stalks celery (about 9 oz./255 g *total*), chopped**
- 1 **clove garlic, minced or pressed**
- 2 **teaspoons dried oregano**
- 2 **cans (about 15 oz./425 g *each*) tomato purée**
- 1 **cup (240 ml) dry red wine**
- 1 **pound (455 g) soft tofu, rinsed and drained**
- 1 **package (about 10 oz./285 g) thawed frozen spinach, squeezed dry**
- 12 **dried manicotti shells (about 6 oz./170 g *total*)**
- ½ **cup (60 g) shredded part-skim mozzarella cheese**

1. Heat oil in a wide nonstick frying pan over medium heat. Add onion, celery, garlic, and oregano. Cook, stirring often, until onion is soft (5 to 8 minutes). Add tomato purée, wine, and 1 cup (240 ml) water. Bring to boil; reduce heat, cover, and simmer, stirring often, for 25 minutes. Meanwhile, mix tofu and spinach in a bowl until well blended. Stuff dried pasta with mixture.

2. Spread 1¾ cups (420 ml) of the tomato sauce in a 9- by 13-inch (23- by 33-cm) baking pan. Arrange pasta in pan. Top with remaining sauce. Cover and bake in a 375°F (190°C) oven until tender when pierced (about 50 minutes). Sprinkle with cheese. Makes 6 servings.

Per serving: 302 calories (25% fat, 57% carbohydrates, 18% protein), 9 g total fat (2 g saturated), 45 g carbohydrates, 14 g protein, 6 mg cholesterol, 692 mg sodium

Orecchiette with Lentils & Goat Cheese

Preparation time: About 10 minutes

Cooking time: About 35 minutes

Tangy goat cheese transforms a savory pasta-lentil mixture into a sprightly main-course offering.

- 2 cups (470 ml) vegetable broth
- 6 ounces/170 g (about 1 cup) lentils, rinsed and drained
- 1 tablespoon chopped fresh thyme or 1 teaspoon dried thyme
- 8 ounces/230 g (about 2⅓ cups) dried orecchiette or other medium-size pasta shape
- ⅓ cup (80 ml) white wine vinegar
- 3 tablespoons chopped parsley
- 2 tablespoons olive oil
- 1 teaspoon honey (or to taste)
- 1 clove garlic, minced or pressed
- ½ cup (65 g) crumbled goat or feta cheese
- Thyme sprigs
- Salt and pepper

1. Bring broth to a boil in a 1½- to 2-quart (1.4- to 1.9-liter) pan over high heat. Add lentils and chopped thyme; reduce heat, cover, and simmer until lentils are tender to bite (20 to 30 minutes). Meanwhile, bring 8 cups (1.9 liters) water to a boil in a 4- to 5-quart (3.8- to 5-liter) pan over medium-high heat. Stir in pasta and cook just until tender to bite (8 to 10 minutes); or cook according to package directions. Drain pasta and, if necessary, lentils well. Transfer pasta and lentils to a large serving bowl; keep warm.

2. Combine vinegar, parsley, oil, honey, and garlic in a small bowl. Beat until blended. Add to pasta mixture and mix thoroughly but gently. Sprinkle with cheese. Garnish with thyme sprigs. Offer salt and pepper to add to taste. Makes 4 servings.

Per serving: 515 calories (24% fat, 57% carbohydrates, 19% protein), 14 g total fat (5 g saturated), 75 g carbohydrates, 25 g protein, 13 mg cholesterol, 604 mg sodium

Artichoke Pesto Pasta

Preparation time: About 15 minutes

Cooking time: About 15 minutes

Artichokes rather than basil star in the nontraditional pesto for this pasta dish.

- ¼ cup (35 g) pine nuts
- 1 can (about 10 oz./285 g) artichoke hearts in water, drained
- ½ cup (40 g) freshly grated Parmesan cheese
- 3 ounces (85 g) Neufchâtel or cream cheese
- ¼ cup (45 g) diced onion
- 1 tablespoon Dijon mustard
- 1 clove garlic, minced or pressed
- ⅛ teaspoon ground nutmeg
- ¾ cup (180 ml) vegetable broth
- 1 pound (455 g) dried fettuccine
- ¼ cup (15 g) minced parsley
- ¼ teaspoon crushed red pepper flakes

1. Toast pine nuts in a small frying pan over medium heat, shaking pan often, until golden (about 3 minutes). Remove from pan and set aside.

2. Combine artichokes, Parmesan, Neufchâtel, onion, mustard, garlic, nutmeg, and ½ cup (120 ml) of the broth in a food processor or blender. Whirl until blended. Set aside.

3. Bring 16 cups (3.8 liters) water to a boil in a 6- to 8-quart (6- to 8-liter) pan over medium-high heat. Stir in pasta and cook just until tender to bite (8 to 10 minutes); or cook according to package directions. Drain well and return to pan. Reduce heat to medium, add remaining ¼ cup (60 ml) broth, and cook, lifting pasta with 2 forks, until broth is hot (about 30 seconds).

4. Transfer to a large serving bowl. Quickly add artichoke mixture, parsley, red pepper flakes, and nuts; lift with 2 forks to mix. Makes 8 servings.

Per serving: 308 calories (26% fat, 57% carbohydrates, 17% protein), 9 g total fat (3 g saturated), 45 g carbohydrates, 13 g protein, 66 mg cholesterol, 343 mg sodium

MACARONI & CHEESE

Pictured on facing page

Preparation time: About 15 minutes

Cooking time: About 1 hour

This creamy, reduced-fat version of the popular casserole substitutes low-fat cottage cheese for some of the Cheddar and nonfat milk for whole milk.

- 2 slices (about 2 oz./55 g *total*) sourdough sandwich bread, torn into pieces
- 1 teaspoon olive oil
- 2 cloves garlic, minced or pressed
- 2 cups (420 g) low-fat (1%) cottage cheese
- 1½ cups (360 ml) nonfat milk
- 1 tablespoon all-purpose flour
- 8 ounces/230 g (about 2 cups) dried elbow macaroni
- 1½ cups (about 6 oz./170 g) grated sharp Cheddar cheese
- ⅛ teaspoon ground nutmeg
  Salt and ground white pepper
  Chopped parsley (optional)

1. Whirl bread in a blender or food processor until fine crumbs form. Combine crumbs, 1 tablespoon water, oil, and garlic in a wide nonstick frying pan. Cook over medium heat, stirring, until crumbs are crisp (8 to 10 minutes). Remove from pan and set aside.

2. Combine cottage cheese and ½ cup (120 ml) of the milk in a blender or food processor. Whirl until smooth; set aside. In a small bowl, whisk flour and ¼ cup (60 ml) more milk until smooth; set aside.

3. Bring 8 cups (1.9 liters) water to a boil in a 4- to 5-quart (3.8- to 5-liter) pan over medium-high heat. Stir in pasta and cook just until tender to bite (8 to 10 minutes); or cook according to package directions. Meanwhile, heat remaining ¾ cup (180 ml) milk in another 4- to 5-quart (3.8- to 5-liter) pan over medium heat until steaming; do not boil. Add flour mixture, whisking until smooth. Cook, stirring often, until mixture begins to thicken (about 2 minutes). Remove from heat and stir in cottage cheese mixture, Cheddar cheese, and nutmeg.

4. Drain pasta well. Add to cheese mixture and mix thoroughly but gently. Season to taste with salt and white pepper. Spoon into a 2- to 2½-quart (1.9- to

2.4-liter) oval casserole. Cover tightly and bake in a 350°F (175°C) oven for 20 minutes. Uncover, sprinkle with crumbs, and continue to bake until top is lightly browned and mixture is bubbling (about 20 more minutes). Let stand for 5 minutes. Sprinkle with parsley, if desired. Makes 4 servings.

Per serving: 554 calories (29% fat, 44% carbohydrates, 27% protein), 18 g total fat (10 g saturated), 60 g carbohydrates, 37 g protein, 51 mg cholesterol, 861 mg sodium

ROTINI WITH BROCCOLI & RICOTTA

Preparation time: About 10 minutes

Cooking time: About 10 minutes

Broccoli adds crunch to this wholesome meatless entrée.

- 12 ounces/340 g (about 5 cups) dried rotini or other corkscrew-shaped pasta
- 2 tablespoons olive oil
- 5 green onions, thinly sliced
- 1 pound (455 g) broccoli flowerets, cut into bite-size pieces
- 1½ cups (345 g) part-skim ricotta cheese
  Freshly grated Parmesan cheese
  Coarsely ground pepper

1. Bring 12 cups (2.8 liters) water to a boil in a 5- to 6-quart (5- to 6-liter) pan over medium-high heat. Stir in pasta and cook just until tender to bite (8 to 10 minutes); or cook according to package directions. Meanwhile, heat oil in a wide nonstick frying pan over medium-high heat. Add onions and cook, stirring, for 1 minute. Add broccoli and continue to cook, stirring, until bright green (about 3 minutes). Pour in ¼ cup (60 ml) water and bring to a boil; reduce heat, cover, and simmer until broccoli is tender-crisp (about 5 minutes).

2. Drain pasta well, reserving ¼ cup (60 ml) of the water. Place in a large serving bowl. Add vegetables and ricotta. Mix thoroughly but gently; if too dry, stir in enough of the reserved water to moisten. Offer Parmesan and pepper to add to taste. Makes 4 servings.

Per serving: 540 calories (26% fat, 55% carbohydrates, 19% protein), 16 g total fat (6 g saturated), 75 g carbohydrates, 25 g protein, 29 mg cholesterol, 149 mg sodium

Macaroni & Cheese (recipe above left) ▶

SPAGHETTI WITH BEANS & SPAGHETTI SQUASH

Preparation time: About 15 minutes

Cooking time: About 1¾ hours

Spaghetti and its vegetable namesake star in this svelte pasta dish. Lima beans add protein.

1	**spaghetti squash (about 2½ lbs./1.15 kg)**
1½	**cups (360 ml) vegetable broth**
1	**package (about 10 oz./285 g) frozen baby lima beans**
2	**tablespoons fresh thyme or 2 teaspoons dried thyme**
1½	**teaspoons grated lemon peel**
8	**cups (440 g) lightly packed spinach leaves, cut into narrow strips**
12	**ounces (340 g) dried spaghetti**
	Salt and pepper

1. Pierce squash shell in several places. Place in a shallow pan slightly larger than squash. Bake in a 350°F (175°C) oven until shell gives readily when pressed (1¼ to 1½ hours).

2. Halve squash lengthwise; remove seeds. Scrape squash from shell, using a fork to loosen strands, and place in a 3- to 4-quart (2.8- to 3.8-liter) pan. Add broth, beans, thyme, and lemon peel. Bring to a boil over high heat; reduce heat, cover, and simmer, stirring often, just until beans are tender to bite (about 5 minutes). Add spinach. Cover and cook until spinach is wilted (1 to 2 more minutes). Remove from heat and keep warm.

3. Bring 12 cups (2.8 liters) water to a boil in a 5- to 6-quart (5- to 6-liter) pan over medium-high heat. Stir in pasta and cook just until tender to bite (8 to 10 minutes); or cook according to package directions. Drain well; return to pan. Add squash mixture and lift with 2 forks to mix. Transfer to a serving bowl. Offer salt and pepper to add to taste. Makes 8 servings.

Per serving: 259 calories (6% fat, 77% carbohydrates, 17% protein), 2 g total fat (0.3 g saturated), 51 g carbohydrates, 11 g protein, 0 mg cholesterol, 284 mg sodium

LINGUINE WITH RED & GREEN SAUCE

Preparation time: About 25 minutes

Cooking time: About 35 minutes

Bell peppers, fresh herbs, and garbanzo beans produce a richly flavored pasta sauce that's very low in fat.

8	**medium-size red bell peppers (about 3 lbs./1.35 kg *total*)**
1	**pound (455 g) dried linguine**
1	**cup (100 g) thinly sliced green onions**
1	**can (about 15 oz./425 g) garbanzo beans, drained**
¾	**cup (30 g) chopped fresh basil or ¼ cup (8 g) dried basil**
1½	**tablespoons chopped fresh tarragon or 1½ teaspoons dried tarragon**
3	**tablespoons capers, drained**
	Salt and pepper

1. Place bell peppers in a 10- by 15-inch (25- by 38-cm) baking pan. Broil about 3 inches (8 cm) below heat, turning as needed, until charred all over (about 15 minutes). Cover with foil and let cool in pan. Pull off and discard skins, stems, and seeds. Chop finely in a food processor or with a knife. Set aside.

2. Bring 16 cups (3.8 liters) water to a boil in a 6- to 8-quart (6- to 8-liter) pan over medium-high heat. Stir in pasta and cook just until tender to bite (8 to 10 minutes); or cook according to package directions. Meanwhile, combine bell peppers, onions, beans, basil, tarragon, and capers in a 3- to 4-quart (2.8- to 3.8-liter) pan. Cook over medium-high heat, stirring often, until steaming (5 to 7 minutes).

3. Drain pasta well and transfer to a wide, shallow serving bowl. Add vegetable mixture and lift with 2 forks to mix. Offer salt and pepper to add to taste. Makes 8 servings.

Per serving: 295 calories (6% fat, 79% carbohydrates, 15% protein), 2 g total fat (0.2 g saturated), 59 g carbohydrates, 11 g protein, 0 mg cholesterol, 151 mg sodium

Tortellini with Roasted Eggplant, Garlic & Pepper

Preparation time: About 25 minutes

Cooking time: 20 to 30 minutes

Garlic lovers will enjoy this light and delicious tortellini entrée.

½ recipe **Roasted Red Bell Peppers (page 53)**
    Balsamic Vinegar Dressing (recipe follows)

3 large heads **garlic** (about 8 oz./230 g *total*), cloves peeled

2 teaspoons **olive oil**

1 pound (455 g) slender **Oriental eggplants,** halved lengthwise and cut into thirds

1 package (about 9 oz./255 g) fresh cheese **tortellini** or **ravioli**

2 tablespoons chopped **parsley**

24 to 32 **spinach** leaves, coarse stems removed, rinsed and crisped
    Salt and **pepper**

1. Prepare Roasted Red Bell Peppers and Balsamic Vinegar Dressing; set aside.

2. Mix garlic and 1 teaspoon of the oil in a lightly oiled square 8-inch (20-cm) baking pan. Rub eggplant skins with remaining 1 teaspoon oil and arrange, skin sides down, in a lightly oiled 10- by 15-inch (25- by 38-cm) baking pan.

3. Bake garlic and eggplants in a 475°F (245°C) oven, switching pan positions halfway through baking, until garlic is tinged with brown (remove cloves as they brown) and eggplants are richly browned and soft when pressed (20 to 30 minutes); if drippings begin to burn, add 4 to 6 tablespoons water, stirring to loosen browned bits. Meanwhile, bring 12 cups (2.8 liters) water to a boil in a 5- to 6-quart (5- to 6-liter) pan over medium-high heat. Stir in pasta and cook just until tender to bite (4 to 6 minutes); or cook according to package directions.

4. Drain pasta well and transfer to a large nonmetal bowl. Add bell peppers, garlic, eggplants, parsley, and dressing. Mix thoroughly but gently. Arrange spinach on individual plates. Spoon on pasta mixture. Offer salt and pepper to add to taste. Makes 4 servings.

BALSAMIC VINEGAR DRESSING. In a small bowl, combine 2 tablespoons **reduced-sodium soy sauce,** 2 teaspoons **balsamic vinegar,** 1 teaspoon **Oriental sesame oil,** and ½ teaspoon **honey.** Beat until blended.

Per serving: 440 calories (17% fat, 65% carbohydrates, 18% protein), 9 g total fat (1 g saturated), 75 g carbohydrates, 21 g protein, 37 mg cholesterol, 911 mg sodium

Penne, Tofu & Asparagus

Preparation time: About 15 minutes

Marinating time: 15 minutes

Cooking time: About 20 minutes

Tofu marinated in a light and refreshing basil-scented vinaigrette gives this pasta entrée a protein boost.

½ cup (120 ml) **seasoned rice vinegar;** or ½ cup (120 ml) **distilled white vinegar** and 4 teaspoons **sugar**

¼ cup (20 g) freshly grated **Parmesan cheese**

3 tablespoons finely chopped fresh **basil** or 1 tablespoon dried **basil**

2 tablespoons **olive oil**

1 tablespoon **Dijon mustard**

1 clove **garlic,** minced or pressed

8 ounces (230 g) regular **tofu,** rinsed and drained, cut into ½-inch (1-cm) cubes

1 pound (455 g) **asparagus,** tough ends removed, cut diagonally into 1½-inch (3.5-cm) pieces

8 ounces/230 g (about 2½ cups) dried **penne**

1. Combine vinegar, cheese, basil, oil, mustard, and garlic in a large serving bowl. Mix well. Add tofu and stir to coat. Cover and let stand for 15 minutes.

2. Bring 12 cups (2.8 liters) water to a boil in a 5- to 6-quart (5- to 6-liter) pan over medium-high heat. Add asparagus and cook until tender when pierced (about 4 minutes). Lift out with a slotted spoon, add to tofu mixture, and keep warm.

3. Stir pasta into boiling water and cook just until tender to bite (8 to 10 minutes); or cook according to package directions. Drain well. Add pasta to tofu and asparagus. Mix thoroughly but gently. Makes 6 servings.

Per serving: 254 calories (28% fat, 55% carbohydrates, 17% protein), 8 g total fat (2 g saturated), 36 g carbohydrates, 11 g protein, 3 mg cholesterol, 539 mg sodium

STUFFED SHELLS WITH ROASTED RED PEPPER SAUCE

Pictured on facing page

Preparation time: About 20 minutes

Cooking time: About 1 hour

A zesty bean mixture fills jumbo pasta shells.

> Roasted Red Pepper Sauce (page 52)
>
> 1 to 2 tablespoons pine nuts
>
> 20 jumbo shell-shaped pasta (about 6⅔ oz./ 190 g *total*)
>
> 1 can (about 15 oz./425 g) garbanzo beans
>
> ¼ cup (10 g) lightly packed fresh basil
>
> 2 tablespoons *each* chopped parsley and lemon juice
>
> 2 teaspoons Oriental sesame oil
>
> 2 cloves garlic
>
> ¼ teaspoon ground cumin
>
> Salt and pepper
>
> Parsley sprigs

1. Prepare Roasted Red Pepper Sauce; set aside. Toast pine nuts in a small frying pan over medium heat, shaking pan often, until golden (about 3 minutes). Remove from pan and set aside.

2. Bring 12 cups (2.8 liters) water to a boil in a 5- to 6-quart (5- to 6-liter) pan over medium-high heat. Stir in pasta and cook just until almost tender (about 8 minutes; do not overcook). Meanwhile, drain beans, reserving liquid. Combine beans, basil, chopped parsley, lemon juice, oil, garlic, and cumin in a blender or food processor. Whirl, adding reserved liquid as necessary, until smooth but thick. Season to taste with salt and pepper.

3. Drain pasta, rinse with cold water, and drain well. Spoon half the red pepper sauce into a shallow 2- to 2½-quart (1.9- to 2.4-liter) casserole. Fill shells with bean mixture and arrange, filled sides up, in sauce. Top with remaining sauce. Cover tightly and bake in a 350°F (175°C) oven until hot (about 40 minutes). Sprinkle with nuts. Garnish with parsley sprigs. Makes 4 servings.

Per serving: 467 calories (17% fat, 68% carbohydrates, 15% protein), 9 g total fat (2 g saturated), 80 g carbohydrates, 17 g protein, 4 mg cholesterol, 424 mg sodium

THAI TOFU & TAGLIATELLE

Preparation time: About 15 minutes

Cooking time: 20 to 25 minutes

Offer this spicy entrée with a cooling cucumber salad.

> 1 cup (240 ml) vegetable broth
>
> 1 cup (200 g) sugar
>
> ¼ cup (60 ml) reduced-sodium soy sauce
>
> 2 tablespoons cider vinegar
>
> 1 tablespoon cornstarch
>
> 2 teaspoons paprika
>
> 1 teaspoon crushed red pepper flakes
>
> 1 teaspoon salad oil
>
> ⅓ cup minced garlic
>
> 8 to 10 ounces (230 to 285 g) dried tagliatelle or fettuccine
>
> 1 pound (455 g) regular tofu, rinsed and drained, cut into ½-inch (1-cm) cubes
>
> 1 large red bell pepper (about 8 oz./230 g), cut into ½-inch (1-cm) pieces
>
> 1 package (about 10 oz./285 g) frozen tiny peas, thawed

1. Combine broth, sugar, soy sauce, vinegar, cornstarch, paprika, and red pepper flakes in a small bowl; mix until well blended. Set aside.

2. Heat oil in a wide nonstick frying pan over medium-high heat. Add garlic and cook, stirring often, until tinged with gold (about 4 minutes; do not scorch); if pan appears dry, stir in water, 1 tablespoon at a time.

3. Add broth mixture. Cook, stirring often, until sauce comes to a boil. Continue to cook until reduced to about 1¼ cups/300 ml (10 to 15 minutes). Meanwhile, bring 12 cups (2.8 liters) water to a boil in a 5- to 6-quart (5- to 6-liter) pan over medium-high heat. Stir in pasta and cook just until tender to bite (8 to 10 minutes); or cook according to package directions. Drain well and transfer to a wide, shallow serving bowl.

4. Combine tofu, bell pepper, peas, and half the sauce in a large bowl. Mix thoroughly but gently. Spoon over pasta. Offer remaining sauce to add to taste. Makes 4 servings.

Per serving: 634 calories (12% fat, 74% carbohydrates, 14% protein), 8 g total fat (1 g saturated), 121 g carbohydrates, 23 g protein, 0 mg cholesterol, 966 mg sodium

◄ **Stuffed Shells with Roasted Red Pepper Sauce (recipe above)**

PASTA SWEETS

Pasta for dessert? Why not, especially when it's sweet noodle pudding or tortellini with a cocoa filling. Offer the noodle pudding, warm or at room temperature, for dessert or as a side dish, as on page 80. If needed, use a round cookie cutter to shape won ton skins for the tortellini. The filling is made with unsweetened cocoa rather than chocolate, giving the same rich flavor without all the fat.

NOODLE PUDDING

Pictured on page 79

Preparation time: About 15 minutes

Cooking time: About 1 hour

Crunch Topping (recipe follows)

5 ounces/140 g (about 4 cups) dried wide egg noodles

1 cup (240 ml) peach or apricot nectar

½ cup (122 g) smooth applesauce

½ cup (105 g) low-fat (1%) cottage cheese

3 tablespoons sugar

2 large egg whites

1 teaspoon cornstarch mixed with 1 tablespoon water

½ cup (75 g) raisins

1. Prepare Crunch Topping; set aside.

2. Bring 8 cups (1.9 liters) water to a boil in a 4- to 5-quart (3.8- to 5-liter) pan over medium-high heat. Stir in pasta and cook just until tender to bite (8 to 10 minutes); or cook according to package directions. Meanwhile, combine nectar, applesauce, cheese, sugar, and egg whites in a blender or food processor. Stir

cornstarch mixture and add to blender. Whirl until smooth.

3. Drain pasta well and transfer to a nonstick or lightly oiled square 8-inch (20-cm) baking pan. Stir in raisins and cheese mixture. Crumble topping over pudding. Bake in a 350°F (175°C) oven until a knife inserted in center comes out clean and top is golden (about 50 minutes). Makes 8 servings.

CRUNCH TOPPING. In a food processor or bowl, combine ⅓ cup (70 g) **sugar,** ¼ cup (60 g) **butter** or margarine, and ½ teaspoon **ground cinnamon.** Whirl or beat well. Add 1½ cups (40 g) **corn flake cereal.** Mix gently. Press into lumps.

Per serving: 257 calories (23% fat, 68% carbohydrates, 9% protein), 7 g total fat (4 g saturated), 45 g carbohydrates, 6 g protein, 33 mg cholesterol, 190 mg sodium

DESSERT TORTELLINI IN GINGERED BROTH

Preparation time: About 45 minutes

Chilling time: At least 30 minutes

Cooking time: About 10 minutes

Cocoa Filling (recipe follows)

56 potsticker (gyoza) or won ton skins (about 10 oz./285 g *total*), cut into 3¼-inch (8.25-cm) rounds

1 large egg white

7½ cups (1.8 liters) white grape juice

3 tablespoons minced crystalized ginger

1. Prepare Cocoa Filling. Lay a wrapper flat, keeping remaining wrappers covered, and place about

1 teaspoon of the filling in center. Moisten edge with egg, fold over filling, and press to seal. Bring pointed ends together, overlapping; moisten ends with egg and press to seal. Lay on a lightly floured baking sheet and cover with plastic wrap. Repeat to use all filling, arranging pasta in a single layer and using 2 baking sheets, if necessary. (At this point, you may refrigerate for up to 4 hours.)

2. Bring 12 cups (2.8 liters) water to a boil in two 5- to 6-quart (5- to 6-liter) pans over medium-high heat. Reduce heat to a gentle boil. Lower half the pasta into each pan; cook just until tender to bite (4 to 5 minutes). If tortellini stick to each other or to pan bottom, stir gently to loosen. Meanwhile, bring grape juice to a boil in a 3- to 4-quart (2.8- to 3.8-liter) pan over high heat. Remove from heat and keep warm.

3. Drain pasta well. Place in individual bowls and add warm grape juice. Just before serving, sprinkle with ginger. Makes 10 servings.

COCOA FILLING. In a bowl, mix ⅓ cup (45 g) chopped **dried apricots,** ½ teaspoon grated **orange peel,** and 3 tablespoons **orange juice.** Let stand, stirring occasionally, until apricots are softened (about 10 minutes). Transfer to a food processor or blender; add 1 cup (230 g) **part-skim ricotta cheese,** ¼ cup (60 ml) **honey,** 3 tablespoons **unsweetened cocoa powder,** and 1 teaspoon **vanilla.** Whirl until smooth. Cover and refrigerate for at least 30 minutes or up to 2 hours.

Per serving: 309 calories (11% fat, 81% carbohydrates, 8% protein), 4 g total fat (2 g saturated), 63 g carbohydrates, 6 g protein, 15 mg cholesterol, 208 mg sodium

SPICY CHILI-MAC

Preparation time: About 15 minutes

Cooking time: About 25 minutes

This hearty pasta and bean stew is sure to become a favorite for cool-weather meals.

2 large carrots (about 8 oz./230 g *total*), chopped

1 large onion (about 8 oz./230 g), coarsely chopped

   About 3½ cups (830 ml) vegetable broth

1 can (about 15 oz./425 g) tomatoes

1 can (about 15 oz./425 g) pinto beans; or 2 cups cooked (about 1 cup/190 g dried) pinto beans

1 can (about 15 oz./425 g) kidney beans; or 2 cups cooked (about 1 cup/185 g dried) kidney beans

3 tablespoons chili powder

8 ounces/230 g (about 2 cups) dried elbow macaroni

   About ½ cup (120 g) plain nonfat yogurt

   Salt and crushed red pepper flakes

1. Combine carrots, onion, and ¼ cup (60 ml) water in a 4- to 5-quart (3.8- to 5-liter) pan. Cook over medium-high heat, stirring often, until liquid has evaporated and vegetables begin to brown (about 10 minutes).

2. Add 3½ cups (830 ml) of the broth and tomatoes and their liquid; break up tomatoes with a spoon. Stir in pinto and kidney beans and their liquid (if using home-cooked beans, add 1 cup/240 ml more broth smoothly blended with 1 teaspoon cornstarch). Add chili powder, stirring to loosen browned bits. Bring to a boil. Stir in pasta and boil gently just until pasta is tender to bite (8 to 10 minutes). If mixture is too thick, add broth; if too thin, continue to simmer until mixture is of desired consistency.

3. Ladle into bowls. Offer yogurt, salt, and red pepper flakes to add to taste. Makes 4 to 6 servings.

Per serving: 399 calories (7% fat, 76% carbohydrates, 17% protein), 3 g total fat (0.3 g saturated), 77 g carbohydrates, 18 g protein, 0.5 mg cholesterol, 1,575 mg sodium

BUCATINI & BLACK BEANS

Preparation time: About 15 minutes

Cooking time: About 20 minutes

Offer this piquant pasta dish with chunks of bread to dunk into any leftover sauce.

10 ounces (285 g) dried bucatini, perciatelli, or spaghetti

⅔ cup (160 ml) seasoned rice vinegar; or ⅔ cup (160 ml) distilled white vinegar and 2 tablespoons sugar

2 tablespoons honey

1 tablespoon olive oil

½ teaspoon chili oil

2 cans (about 15 oz./425 g *each*) black beans, drained and rinsed, or 4 cups cooked (about 2 cups/400 g dried) black beans, drained and rinsed

4 large pear-shaped (Roma-type) tomatoes (about 12 oz./340 g *total*), diced

⅓ cup (20 g) finely chopped parsley

¼ cup (25 g) thinly sliced green onions

¾ cup (100 g) crumbled feta cheese (or to taste)

   Parsley sprigs

1. Bring 12 cups (2.8 liters) water to a boil in a 5- to 6-quart (5- to 6-liter) pan over medium-high heat. Stir in pasta and cook just until tender to bite (10 to 12 minutes); or cook according to package directions. Drain well and keep warm.

2. Combine vinegar, honey, olive oil, and chili oil in pan. Bring just to a boil over medium-high heat. Add pasta, beans, and tomatoes. Cook, stirring, until hot. Remove from heat; stir in chopped parsley and onions.

3. Spoon pasta mixture into bowls. Sprinkle with cheese. Garnish with parsley sprigs. Makes 4 servings.

Per serving: 564 calories (18% fat, 67% carbohydrates, 15% protein), 11 g total fat (5 g saturated), 96 g carbohydrates, 21 g protein, 23 mg cholesterol, 1,095 mg sodium

INDEX

Salmon with Asian-style Capellini ▶
(recipe on page 57)

ACKNOWLEDGMENTS

We thank Linda Selden and the National Pasta Association
for their help in preparing the manuscript. We are also grateful to
R. H. and Fillamento for supplying props used in the photography.